# PHILIP'S

CW00418643

# STR... ...S

# York

www.philips-maps.co.uk

First published 2002 by

Philip's, a division of
Octopus Publishing Group Ltd
www.octopusbooks.co.uk
2–4 Heron Quays
London E14 4JP
An Hachette Livre UK Company
www.hachettelivre.co.uk

Second edition 2007
Second impression with revisions 2008

ISBN 978-0-540-09041-9

© Philip's 2008

**Ordnance Survey®**

This product includes mapping data
licensed from Ordnance Survey®, with the
permission of the Controller of Her Majesty's
Stationery Office.© Crown copyright 2008.
All rights reserved.
Licence number 100011710

Photographs on pages VI and VII:
James Hughes

Printed by Toppan, China

## Contents

**II** **Key to map symbols**

**III** **Key to map pages**

**IV** **Route planning**

**VI** **Sights of York**

**2** **Street maps** at 2¼ inches to 1 mile

**39** **Street maps** at 4½ inches to 1 mile

**64** **Street maps of York city centre** at 7 inches to 1 mile

**66** **Index**

**73** **List of numbered locations**

# Key to map symbols

## Roads

| | |
|---|---|
| **(12)** | **Motorway** with junction number |
| **A42** | **Primary route** – dual, single carriageway |
| **A42** | **A road** – dual, single carriageway |
| **B1289** | **B road** – dual, single carriageway |
| | **Through-route** – dual, single carriageway |
| | **Minor road** – dual, single carriageway |
| | **Rural track, private road or narrow road in urban area** |
| | **Path, bridleway, byway open to all traffic, road used as a public path** |
| | **Road under construction** |
| | **Pedestrianised area** |
| | **Gate or obstruction to traffic** restrictions may not apply at all times or to all vehicles |
| **P** **P&R** | **Parking, Park and Ride** |

## Railways

| | |
|---|---|
| | **Railway** |
| | **Miniature railway** |
| | **Metro station, private railway station** |

## Emergency services

| | |
|---|---|
| | **Ambulance station, coastguard station** |
| | **Fire station, police station** |
| **H** **+** | **Hospital, Accident and Emergency entrance to hospital** |

## General features

| | |
|---|---|
| **+** **PO** | **Place of worship, Post Office** |
| **i** | **Information centre** (open all year) |
| | **Bus or coach station, shopping centre** |
| | **Important buildings,** schools, colleges, universities and hospitals |
| | **Woods, built-up area** |
| *Tumulus* FORT | **Non-Roman antiquity, Roman antiquity** |

## Leisure facilities

| | |
|---|---|
|   | **Camping site, caravan site** |
| | **Golf course, picnic site** |

## Boundaries

| | |
|---|---|
| ● ● ● ● ● ● ● ● | **Postcode boundaries** |
| ▬▬▬ · ▬▬▬ | **County and unitary authority boundaries** |

## Water features

| | |
|---|---|
| River Ouse | **Tidal water, water name** |
| | **Non-tidal water** – lake, river, canal or stream |
| ◁ ─┤ | **Lock, weir** |

## Enlarged mapping only

| | |
|---|---|
| | **Railway or bus station building** |
|  | **Place of interest, parkland** |

## Scales

**Green pages: 2¼ inches to 1 mile** 1:28 160
| 0 | ¼ mile | ½ mile | ¾ mile | 1 mile |
| 0 | 250m | 500m | 750m | 1 km |

**Blue pages: 4½ inches to 1 mile** 1:14 080
| 0 | 220 yds | ¼ mile | 660 yds | ½ mile |
| 0 | 125m | 250m | 375m | ½ km |

**Red pages: 7 inches to 1 mile** 1:9051
| 0 | 110 yds | 220 yds | 330 yds | ¼ mile |
| 0 | 125m | 250m | 375m | ½km |

**44** **Adjoining page indicators** The colour of the arrow and the band indicates the scale of the adjoining page (see above)

## Abbreviations

| | | | | |
|---|---|---|---|---|
| Acad | **Academy** | Mkt | **Market** |
| Allot Gdns | **Allotments** | Meml | **Memorial** |
| Cemy | **Cemetery** | Mon | **Monument** |
| C Ctr | **Civic Centre** | Mus | **Museum** |
| CH | **Club House** | Obsy | **Observatory** |
| Coll | **College** | Pal | **Royal Palace** |
| Crem | **Crematorium** | PH | **Public House** |
| Ent | **Enterprise** | Recn Gd | **Recreation Ground** |
| Ex H | **Exhibition Hall** | Resr | **Reservoir** |
| Ind Est | **Industrial Estate** | Ret Pk | **Retail Park** |
| IRB Sta | **Inshore Rescue Boat Station** | Sch | **School** |
| | | Sh Ctr | **Shopping Centre** |
| Inst | **Institute** | TH | **Town Hall/House** |
| Ct | **Law Court** | Trad Est | **Trading Estate** |
| L Ctr | **Leisure Centre** | Univ | **University** |
| LC | **Level Crossing** | Wks | **Works** |
| Liby | **Library** | YH | **Youth Hostel** |

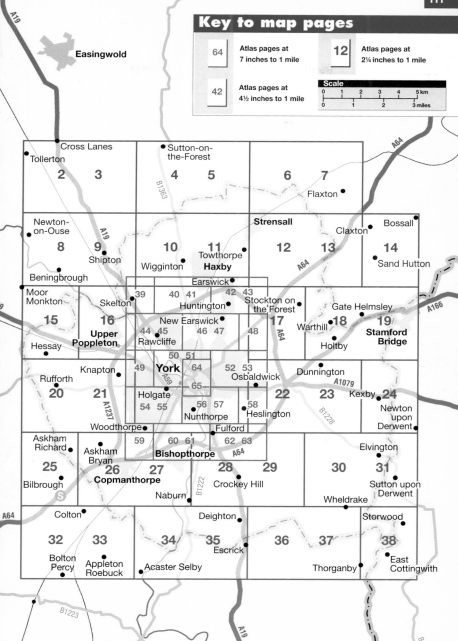

III

## Key to map pages

| 64 | Atlas pages at 7 inches to 1 mile |
| 12 | Atlas pages at 2¼ inches to 1 mile |
| 42 | Atlas pages at 4½ inches to 1 mile |

**Scale**
0  1  2  3  4  5 km
0      1      2      3 miles

Easingwold

A19

Cross Lanes
Tollerton
**2**   **3**

Sutton-on-the-Forest
**4**   **5**

**6**   **7**
Flaxton

A64

Newton-on-Ouse
**8**   **9**
Shipton

**Strensall**

**10**   **11**
Wigginton   Towthorpe   **Haxby**

**12**   **13**
Claxton   Bossall

**14**
Sand Hutton

Beningbrough
Moor Monkton
**15**   **16**
Skelton
**Upper Poppleton**
Hessay

Earswick
**39**
**40**  **41**   **42**  **43**
Huntington   Stockton on the Forest
New Earswick
**44**  **45**   **46**  **47**   **48**
Rawcliffe

**17**
Warthill   **18**
Holtby
Gate Helmsley
**19**
**Stamford Bridge**

A166

Knapton
Rufforth
**20**   **21**

**50**  **51**
**49**   **York**   **64**
Holgate
**54**  **55**
Woodthorpe

**52**  **53**
Osbaldwick
**65**
**56**  **57**
Nunthorpe
**58**
Heslington
**Fulford**

**22**   **23**
Dunnington
A1079   Kexby   **24**
Newton upon Derwent

Askham Richard
**25**
Bilbrough

Askham Bryan
**26**
**Copmanthorpe**

**59**
**60**  **61**
**Bishopthorpe**
**27**
**62**  **63**
A64

**28**   **29**
Crockey Hill
Naburn

Elvington
**30**   **31**
Sutton upon Derwent
Wheldrake

Colton
**32**   **33**
Bolton Percy   Appleton Roebuck   Acaster Selby

**34**   **35**
Deighton
Escrick

**36**   **37**
Thorganby

Storwood
**38**
East Cottingwith

A64

B1222
B1223

A19   A163   B1228

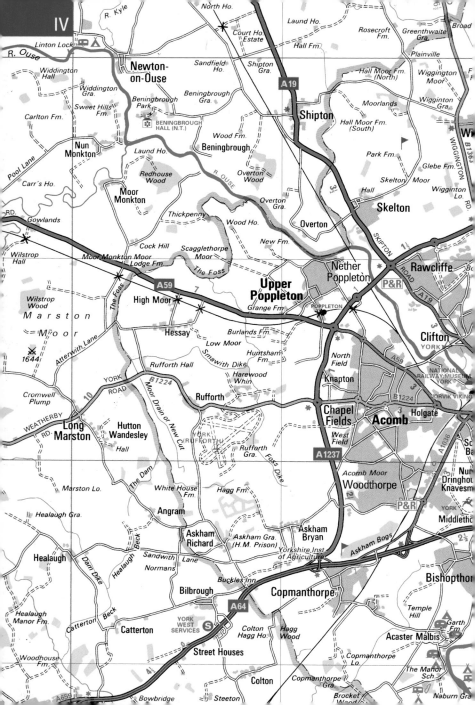

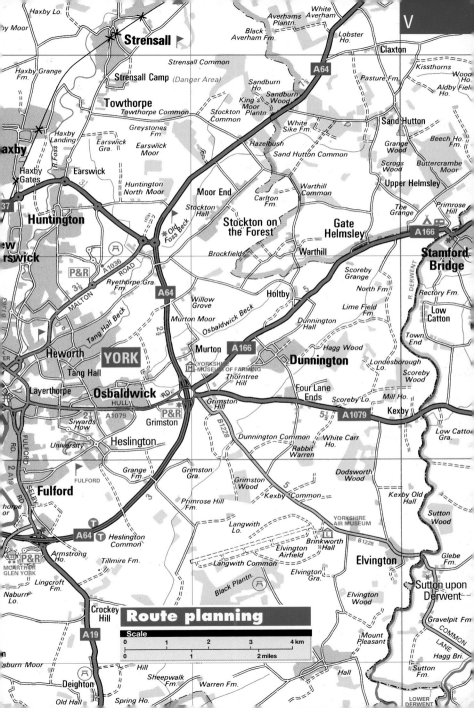

# Sights of York

## Museums and Galleries

**The Bar Convent Museum** *Blossom Street* Early history of Christianity in the north of England. 🖥www.bar-convent.org.uk 📞01904 643238 **65 A1**

**Jorvik Viking Centre**★★ *Coppergate* Reconstruction and artefacts from the Viking village Jorvik based on archaeological finds in York. 🖥www.vikingjorvik.com 📞01904 543400 **65 B2**

**Micklegate Bar Museum** *On the Bar Walls* Over 800 years of York. 📞01904 634436 🖥www.micklegatebar.co.uk **65 A1**

**National Railway Museum**★★ *Leeman Road* Largest railway museum in the world. Collection includes Royal trains, record breaking Mallard locomotive and a replica of Stephenson's Rocket. 📞01904 621261 🖥www.nrm.org.uk **50 C1**

**Regimental Museum** *Tower Street* History of two of Yorkshire's famous regiments, the Royal Dragoon Guards, and the Prince of Wales's Own Regiment of Yorkshire. 🖥www.armymuseums.org.uk 📞01904 642036/461010 **65 B1**

**Richard III Museum** *Monk Bar Gatehouse* Exhibition tells the story of Richard III, (King of England 1483-85). 📞01904 634191 🖥www.richard3museum.co.uk **64 C3**

**York Art Gallery**★ *Exhibition Square* 600 years of painting housed in 19th-century Italian Renaissance-style building. 📞01904 687687 🖥www.yorkartgallery.org.uk **64 B3**

**York Castle Museum**★ *The Castle, off Tower Street.* Everyday life as a Victorian, with shops, parlours, prisons and a mill house. Play Victorian games and walk cobbled streets with costumed characters. 📞01904 687687 🖥www.yorkcastlemuseum.org.uk **65 C1**

**York Dungeon** *Clifford Street* Museum of horror. 🖥www.thedungeons.com 📞01904 632599 **65 B2**

**Yorkshire Air Museum**★ *Halifax Way, Elvington* Preserved wartime airfield with aircraft, including the only complete Halifax in the world. 🖥www.yorkshireairmuseum.co.uk 📞01904 608595 **30 B4**

**Yorkshire Museum**★ *Museum Gardens* Covers 1000 years of Yorkshire's heritage. 🖥www.yorkshiremuseum.org.uk 📞01904 687687 **64 A3**

**Yorkshire Museum of Farming** *Murton Park, Murton* Archives, exhibits and farm vehicle displays. 🖥www.murtonpark.co.uk 📞01904 489966 **22 C4**

## Historic Sites

**Bedern Hall** *Bartle Garth, St Andrewgate* 14th-century former refectory of the Vicars Choral, now used as a function room. 📞01904 653698 🖥www.bedernhall.co.uk **64 C3**

**Eboracum Legion Bathhouse** *St Sampsons Square* Pub with a Roman bath in basement – discovered during renovation. Can be viewed from a suspended walkway. 📞01904 620455 🖥www.yorkromanbath.co.uk **65 B2**

**Grand Assembly Rooms** *Blake Street* Historic building, currently leased as a restaurant. Available to view during restaurant opening hours. 🖥www.visityork.org 📞01904 637254 **64 B3**

**The Guildhall** *St Helens Square* Replica of the 15th-century building, the original was destroyed by fire in an air raid in 1942. 📞01904 551049 🖥www.york.gov.uk **65 B2**

**The King's Manor**★ *Exhibition Square* Historic building owned by the University of York. 16th-century seat of the Council of the North. 🖥www.york.ac.uk **64 B3**

**Mansion House** *St Helens Square* Georgian house, home to the city's Lord Mayors since the 18th century. Open for tours. 📞01904 552036 🖥www.york.gov.uk **65 B2**

**Merchant Adventurers' Hall**★ *Fossgate* Built 1350s. Possibly Europe's finest medieval guildhall. 🖥www.theyorkcompany.co.uk 📞01904 654818 **65 C2**

**Merchant Taylors' Hall** *Aldwark* Fine 14th-century craft guildhall with medieval roof. 📞01904 624889 🖥www.thisisyork.co.uk **64 C3**

**St Anthony's Hall** *Peasholme Green* Partly 15th century. Now the Borthwick Institute of Historical Research at the University of York. Open to the public. 🖥www.york.ac.uk 📞01904 642315 **65 C2**

**St William's College** *College Street* Timbered 15th-century building, originally college for Minster Chantry priests. Medieval halls open to view. Now home to York Minster Information & Conference Centre and a restaurant. 🖥www.yorkminster.org 📞01904 557233 **64 B3**

## Houses

**Barley Hall** *Coffee Yard* Restored medieval merchant's house, home to Alderman Snawsell. 🖥www.barleyhall.org.uk 📞01904 610275 **64 B3**

**Beningbrough Hall and Gardens**★ *Beningbrough* Baroque house. Contains portraits loaned by the National Portrait Gallery. Gardens and parkland. 📞01904 472027 🖥www.nationaltrust.org.uk **8 A2**

**Bishopthorpe Palace** *Bishopthorpe Road* Official home of Archbishop of York in 9 acres of grounds. Only open for pre-booked groups. 🖥www.dioceseofyork.org.uk 📞01904 707021 **61 A1**

**Brockfield Hall** *Warthill* Georgian country house. Limited opening throughout August, appointment only all other times. 🖥www.historichousevenues.com 📞01904 489362 **18 A3**

**Fairfax House** *Castlegate* 18th-century town house, with Noel Terry furniture collection. 🖥www.fairfaxhouse.co.uk 📞01904 655543 **65 B2**

**Sutton Park**★ *Sutton-on-the-Forest* Early Georgian house built 1730. Gardens overlook spacious parkland. 📞01347 810249 🖥www.statelyhome.co.uk **4 B4**

**Treasurer's House**★ *Minster Yard* 17th–18th-century town house, with four centuries of styles on display. Tearoom. 📞01904 624247 🖥www.nationaltrust.org.uk **64 B3**

## City Defences

**Bar Walls** *Around central York* (also known as the City Walls) There have been defensive walls surrounding York since Roman times. The walls have since been demolished in places and added to, but some Roman masonry can be found in their foundations. They are named 'Bar Walls' after their gates, or bars, used for entry to and defence of the city. Micklegate bar is the largest surviving gatehouse. 🖥www.york.gov.uk/walls **64 B3**

**Bootham Bar** *High Petergate* Stands on the site of former Roman gateway and has some of earliest medieval stonework on the walls. 🖥www.york.gov.uk/walls **64 B3**

▼ **York Minster seen from the city wall near Monk Bar**

**Clifford's Tower**★ *Tower Street* Built around 1250 at the same time as the castle. The Lancastrian leader Roger de Clifford was hanged here in 1322 for opposing Edward II. 🖳 www.cliffordstower.com 65 B1

**Fishergate Postern Tower** *Piccadilly* Built between 1504 and 1507. 🖳 www.york.gov.uk/walls 65 C1

**Micklegate Bar**★ *Micklegate* The 12th-century royal gateway to York, the portcullis was added in 14th century. The site where traitors' heads were displayed and civic ceremonies took place. 🖳 www.york.gov.uk/walls 65 A1

**Monk Bar**★ *Goodramgate* Built in 14th century, still with operational portcullis. Houses Richard III museum. 🖳 www.york.gov.uk/walls 64 C3

**Multangular Tower** *Museum Gardens* Built as part of Roman defences, probably around 210, only part of the remaining tower is Roman. 🖳 www.york.gov.uk/walls 64 A3

**The Red Tower** *Navigation Road* Built in 15th century and used as a stable in 18th century. The only brick tower. 🖳 www.york.gov.uk/walls 52 A1

**Robin Hood Tower** *Lord Mayors Walk* Built by the Victorians on the site of previous towers in the style of a medieval tower. 🖳 www.york.gov.uk/walls 64 B3

**St Mary's Tower** *Bootham* Built in 14th century and rebuilt after the Civil War. 🖳 www.york.gov.uk/walls 64 A3

**Victoria Bar** *Victoria Street* Opened 1838 in response to population growth. 🖳 www.york.gov.uk/walls 65 B1

**Walmgate Bar** Rectangular two-storey gatehouse. The only bar still to have both the portcullis and barbican and the wooden doors. 🖳 www.york.gov.uk/walls 57 A4

**York Castle**★ *Tower Street* Original castle built in 1068 by William the Conqueror but rebuilt in 13th century. After the Civil War it became a prison; some prison buildings remain. 🖳 www.york.gov.uk/walls 65 C1

## Places of Worship

**York Minster**★★ *Deangate* Largest medieval cathedral in Northern Europe, it took over 250 years to build. Octagonal chapter house. Undercroft treasury and crypt with Roman, Saxon and Norman remains. Crypt contains parts of the original Norman cathedral and the coffin of St William. 📞 01904 557216 🖳 www.yorkminster.org 64 B3

**All Saints**★ *North Street* Medieval stained glass windows. 📞 01904 706047 🖳 www.allsaints-northstreet.org.uk 65 B2

**All Saints** *Pavement* Regimental Church of The Royal Dragoon Guards. Tower with octagonal lantern. 🖳 www.rdgmuseum.org.uk/allsaints.htm 📞 01904 624036 65 B2

**Holy Trinity**★ *Goodramgate* In quiet churchyard. 15th-century stained glass, Jacobean box pews. 📞 01904 613451 64 B3

**Holy Trinity** *Micklegate* Medieval church containing the city's stocks. 65 A2

**St Cuthberts** *Peasholme Green* Oldest church in York after the Minster. The walls include some Roman stone. 📞 01904 624190 64 C3

**St Denys** *Walmgate* Old church with Norman porch and rare glass. 📞 01904 633261 65 C2

**St Mary's Abbey** *Museum Gardens* The 11th-century abbey was replaced by a new Gothic church in the 13th century. The impressive ruins of the church can be seen in the Museum Gardens. 📞 01904 643238 64 A3

**St Martin-le-Grand**★ *Coney Street* Badly bombed 15th-century church, restored in 1960s. Shrine to dead of both world wars. 📞 01904 625186 65 B2

**St Michael-le-Belfrey** *Minster Yard* Dating back to 1570, it contains baptism register for Guy Fawkes. 🖳 www.stmichaelsyork.org 📞 01904 624190 64 B3

## Other Sights

**Goodramgate** Lady Row dates from the 14th century. Now houses small collection of shops. 64 B3

**Lendal Tower** *Lendal Bridge* The tower at the eastern end of Lendal Bridge originally served as a defence but was adapted to a waterworks in 17th century. 65 A2

**Newgate Market** *Off Parliament Street* Fresh produce market open daily 8am–5pm. 🖳 www.york.gov.uk/markets 📞 01904 551355 65 B2

**Norwich Union Yorkshire Wheel** *Leeman Road* Unique view of York, towering 60 metres above the city. 🖳 www.nrm.org.uk 📞 01904 621261 50 C1

**The Shambles**★ One of the best preserved medieval streets in Europe. Some of the buildings date back to 1350. 🖳 www.yorkshambles.com 65 B2

**University of York** *Heslington* Established in 1963. The university owns a number of important and historic buildings in the city. (See King's Manor.) 🖳 www.york.ac.uk 📞 01904 430000 57 C2

**York Racecourse** *Knavesmire* Top class horse racing from May to October. 📞 01904 620911 🖳 www.yorkracecourse.co.uk 55 C1

## Green Spaces

**Museum Gardens**★ *Museum Street* Yorkshire Museum set in 10 acres of botanical gardens. 🖳 www.york.gov.uk 📞 01904 551800 64 A3

**Rowntree Park** *Terry Avenue* 20 acres of parkland on the River Ouse. 🖳 www.york.gov.uk 56 B3

**War Memorial Gardens** *Leeman Road* Parkland and memorial. 🖳 www.york.gov.uk 65 A2

**West Bank Park** *Acomb* Park and formal gardens. 🖳 www.york.gov.uk 55 A4

## Activities

**The Archaeological Resource Centre (ARC)**★ *St Saviours Church, St Saviourgate* Linked to the Jorvik Viking Centre. Handle and examine archaeological finds with archaeologist staff.

▲ *Low Petergate*

🖳 www.yorkarchaeology.co.uk 📞 01904 543403 65 C2

**Grand Opera House** *Cumberland Street* Venue for a variety of events including shows, musicals, ballets etc. 📞 01904 671818 🖳 www.york.gov.uk 65 B2

**National Centre for Early Music** *St Margaret's Church, Walmgate* Centre for the study of early music. Venue for concerts, drama performances and workshops. 📞 01904 632220 🖳 www.ncem.co.uk 65 C2

**York Brewery Tour** *Toft Green, Micklegate* Independent brewery, beer is brewed using traditional methods. Daily guided tours around the brewery. 📞 01904 621162 🖳 www.yorkbrew.demon.co.uk 65 A2

**York Model Railway** *Tea Room Square, York Station* 323 metres of Hornby track with up to 14 trains running daily. 📞 01904 630169 🖳 www.cityofyork.com 65 A2

**York Theatre Royal** *St Leonard's Place* Much of present building dates from 19th century although the theatre dates back to 1744. 🖳 www.yorktheatreroyal.co.uk 📞 01904 623568 64 B3

## Information

**Tourist Information**
🛈 York: The De Grey Rooms, Exhibition Square 📞 01904 550099/77 64 B3
🛈 Railway Station: Outer Concourse, Station Road 📞 01904 550099 65 A2

**City of York Council**
The Guildhall 📞 01904 613161 🖳 www.york.gov.uk

**Car Parking City Council**
📞 01904 613161 🖳 www.york.gov.uk

**Car Parking NCP**
📞 0870 606 7050 🖳 www.ncp.co.uk

**National Rail Enquiries**
📞 0845 748 4950 🖳 www.nationalrail.co.uk

**Local Bus and Rail**
📞 0870 608 2608 🖳 www.traveline.org.uk

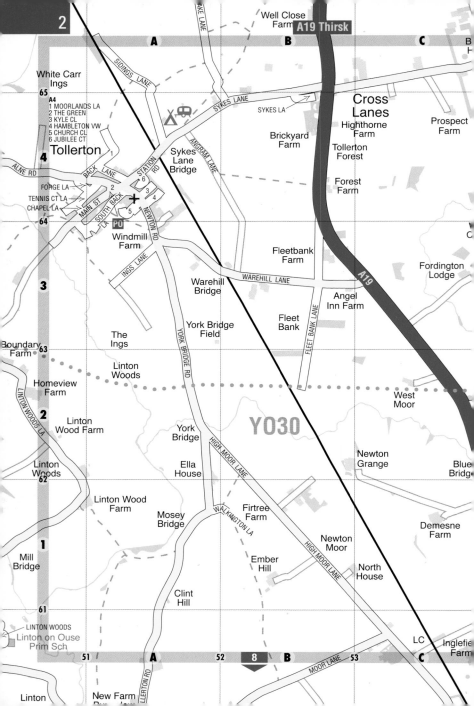

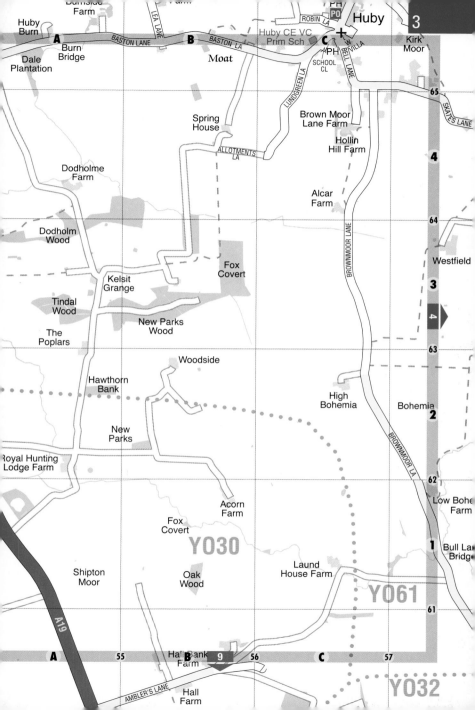

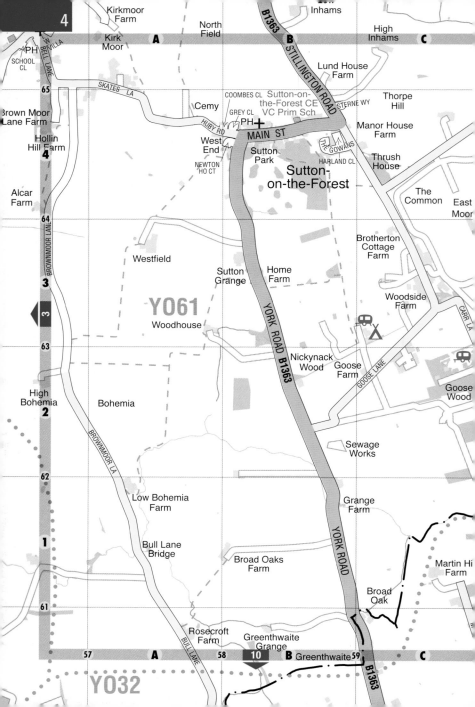

Kirkmoor Farm

North Field

Inhams

High Inhams

B1363

STILLINGTON ROAD

Kirk Moor

PH

BEVILLA

BELL LANE

SCHOOL CL

Lund House Farm

65

SKATES LA

Cemy

COOMBES CL

Sutton-on-the-Forest CE VC Prim Sch

STERNE WY

Thorpe Hill

Brown Moor Lane Farm

GREY CL

PH

Manor House Farm

HUBY RD

West End

MAIN ST

THE GOWANS

Hollin Hill Farm

4

NEWTON HO CT

Sutton Park

HARLAND CL

Thrush House

Alcar Farm

Sutton-on-the-Forest

64

BROWNMOOR LANE

The Common

East Moor

Westfield

Sutton Grange

Home Farm

Brotherton Cottage Farm

3

3

Woodhouse

Woodside Farm

CARR LA

63

Nickynack Wood

Goose Farm

GOOSE LANE

High Bohemia

2

Bohemia

Goose Wood

YO61

BROWNMOOR LA

Sewage Works

62

Low Bohemia Farm

1

Bull Lane Bridge

Broad Oaks Farm

Grange Farm

Martin Hi Farm

61

Broad Oak

BULL LANE

Rosecroft Farm

Greenthwaite Grange

Greenthwaite

B1363

YO32

YORK ROAD

B1363

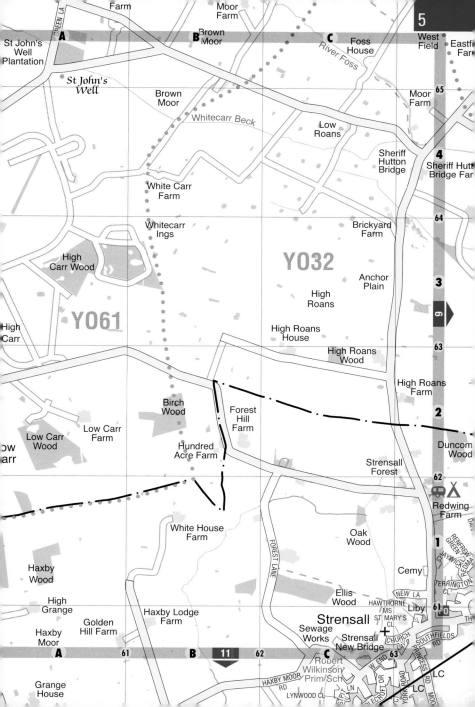

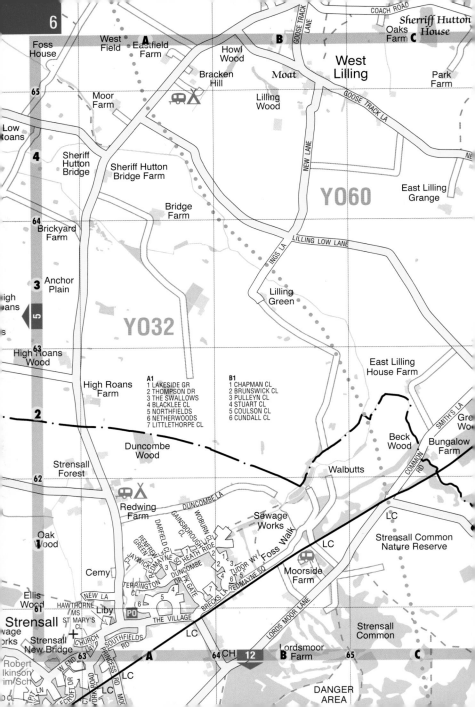

COACH ROAD

**Sheriff Hutton**
**House**

West Field

Foss House

**A**

Eastfield Farm

Howl Wood

**B**

GOOSE TRACK LANE

Oaks Farm **C**

Moat

West Lilling

Bracken Hill

Moor Farm

Lilling Wood

GOOSE TRACK LA

Park Farm

65

Low Roans

**4**

Sheriff Hutton Bridge

Sheriff Hutton Bridge Farm

NEW LANE

YO60

East Lilling Grange

NE

Bridge Farm

64

Brickyard Farm

LILLING LOW LANE

INGS LA

**3**

Anchor Plain

igh oans

**5**

Lilling Green

63

High Roans Wood

YO32

East Lilling House Farm

High Roans Farm

A1
1 LAKESIDE GR
2 THOMPSON DR
3 THE SWALLOWS
4 BLACKLEE CL
5 NORTHFIELDS
6 NETHERWOODS
7 LITTLETHORPE CL

B1
1 CHAPMAN CL
2 BRUNSWICK CL
3 PULLEYN CL
4 STUART CL
5 COULSON CL
6 CUNDALL CL

SMITHS LA

Gre Wo

**2**

Duncombe Wood

Beck Wood

Bungalow Farm

Strensall Forest

62

Walbutts

COMMON RD

Redwing Farm

DUNCOMBE LA

Sewage Works

Foss Walk

LC

Strensall Common Nature Reserve

Oak Wood

GAINSBOROUGH CL

WOBURN CL

HEATH RIDE

DARFIELD CL
REMFRY GREEN
JAYWICK CL

DUNCOMBE DR PK GATE

TUDOR WY

REDMAYNE SQ

BRECKS LA

LC

LORDS MOOR LANE

Moorside Farm

Cemy

TERRINGTON CL

Ellis Wood

61

NEW LA

HAWTHORNE MS
ST MARY'S CL

Liby

**P**

THE VILLAGE

LC

Strensall Common

Strensall

avage orks

Strensall New Bridge

CHURCH

SOUTHFIELDS RD

PRINCESS RD

MOOR

W END LA

63

**A**

64 CH **12** **B** Lordsmoor Farm

65

**C**

Robert kinson m/Sch

TOFTCROFT DR

LN

LC

RD

DANGER AREA

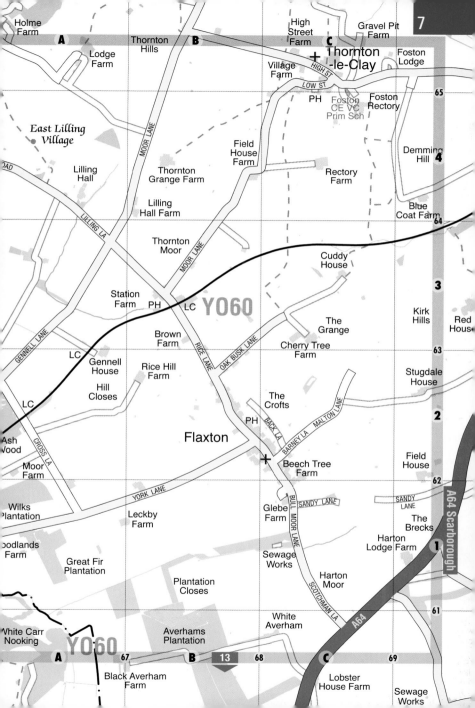

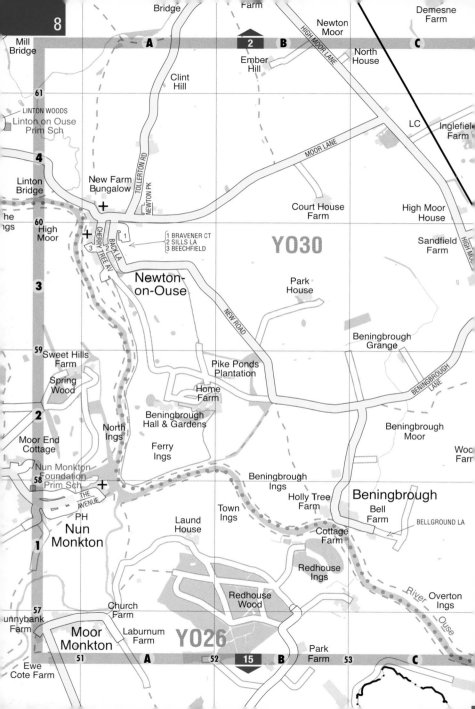

Mill
Bridge

Bridge

Farm

Demesne
Farm

Newton
Moor

**2**

North
House

Ember
Hill

LC

Inglefield
Farm

61

LINTON WOODS
Linton on Ouse
Prim Sch

Clint
Hill

MOOR LANE

HIGH MOOR LANE

4

Linton
Bridge

New Farm
Bungalow

Court House
Farm

High Moor
House

High Mo

60

High
Moor

Newton-
on-Ouse

1 BRAVENER CT
2 SILLS LA
3 BEECHFIELD

YO30

Sandfield
Farm

1
2
3

BACK LA

CHERRY TREE AV

NEWTON PK

TOLLERTON RD

3

Park
House

NEW ROAD

Beningbrough
Grange

59

Sweet Hills
Farm

Pike Ponds
Plantation

BENINGBROUGH LANE

Spring
Wood

Home
Farm

2

Moor End
Cottage

North
Ings

Beningbrough
Hall & Gardens

Beningbrough
Moor

Woo
Farr

Ferry
Ings

Nun Monkton
Foundation
Prim Sch

58

Beningbrough
Ings

Beningbrough

THE AVENUE

Holly Tree
Farm

Bell
Farm

BELLGROUND LA

PH

Town
Ings

Laund
House

Cottage
Farm

1

Nun
Monkton

Redhouse
Ings

River Ouse

Overton
Ings

57

Church
Farm

Redhouse
Wood

unnybank
Farm

Moor
Monkton

Laburnum
Farm

YO26

Park
Farm

51

**A**

52

**15**

**B**

53

**C**

Ewe
Cote Farm

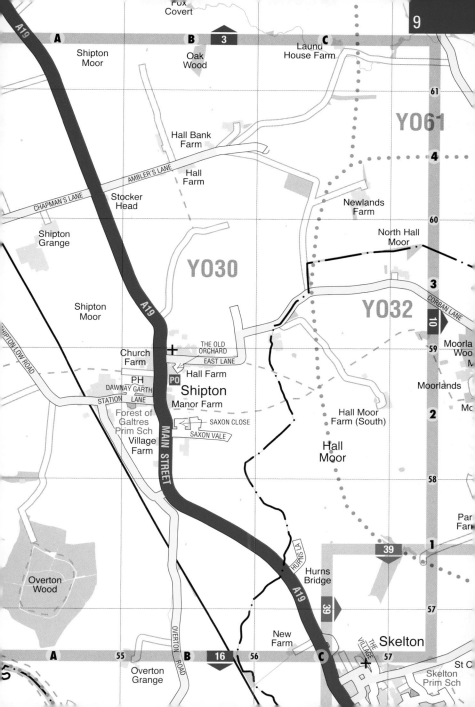

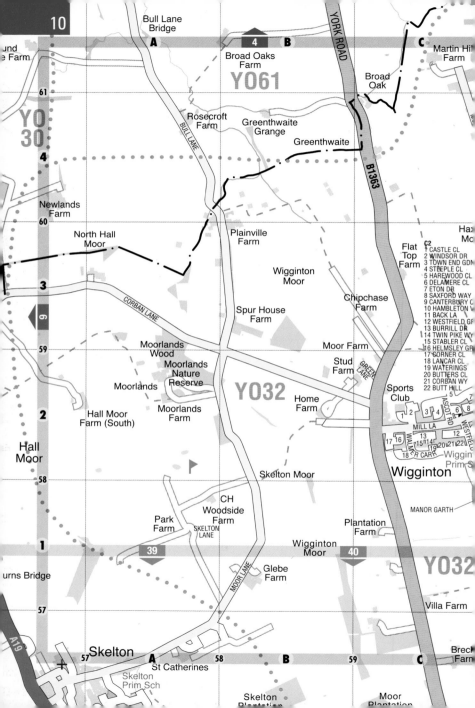

10

Bull Lane
Bridge

A

4

B

York Road

C

Martin Hill
Farm

Broad Oaks
Farm

YO61

Broad
Oak

Greenthwaite

61

YO
30

Rosecroft
Farm

Greenthwaite
Grange

Bull Lane

B1363

4

Newlands
Farm

60

North Hall
Moor

Plainville
Farm

Flat
Top
Farm

C2
1 CASTLE CL
2 WINDSOR DR
3 TOWN END GDN
4 STEEPLE CL
5 HAREWOOD CL
6 DELAMERE CL
7 ETON DR
8 SAXFORD WAY
9 CANTERBURY C
10 HAMBLETON W
11 BACK LA
12 WESTFIELD GR
13 BURRILL DR
14 TWIN PIKE WY
15 STABLER CL
16 HELMSLEY GR
17 CORNER CL
18 LANCAR CL
19 WATERINGS
20 BUTTERS CL
21 CORBAN WY
22 BUTT HILL

Wigginton
Moor

3

6

Corban Lane

Spur House
Farm

Chipchase
Farm

59

Moorlands
Wood

Moorlands
Nature
Reserve

Moor Farm

Stud
Farm

Green Lane

Sports
Club

Tascot Rd

5

Moorlands

YO32

Home
Farm

1 2

3 4 6 7 8

Mill La

Westfiel

2

Hall Moor
Farm (South)

Moorlands
Farm

17 16

13
15 14

12

18 Walmer Carr

11 9 20 21 22

Wiggin
Prim S

Hall
Moor

58

Skelton Moor

Wigginton

Manor Garth

CH
Woodside
Farm

Plantation
Farm

1

Park
Farm

Skelton
Lane

39

Wigginton
Moor

40

YO32

urns Bridge

Glebe
Farm

Moor Lane

57

Villa Farm

A19

57

Skelton

A

58

B

59

C

Brec
Farm

St Catherines

Skelton
Prim Sch

Skelton
Plantation

Moor
Plantation

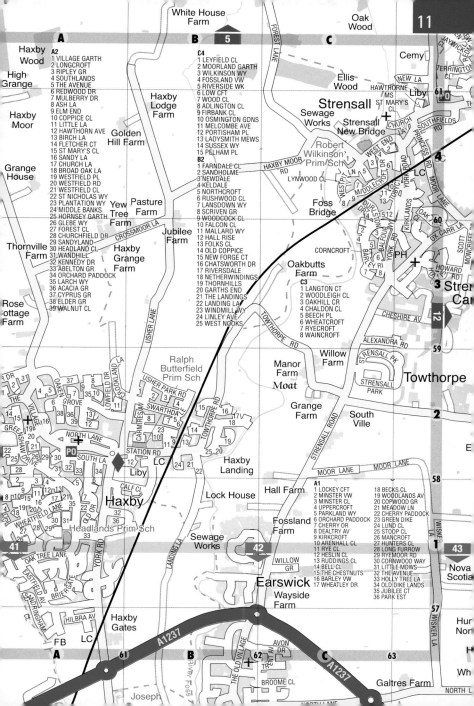

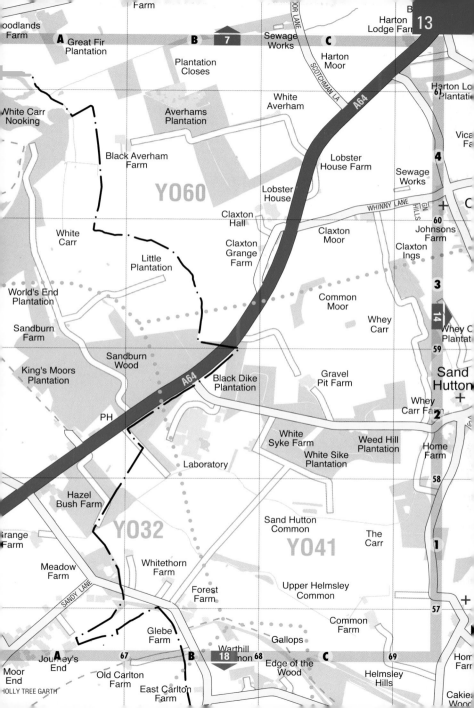

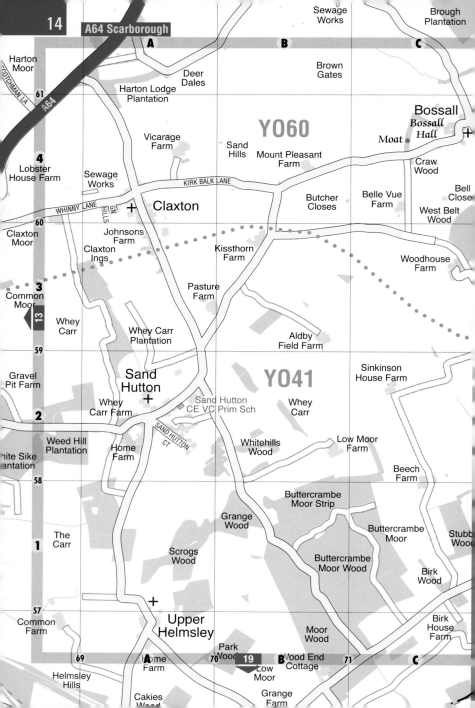

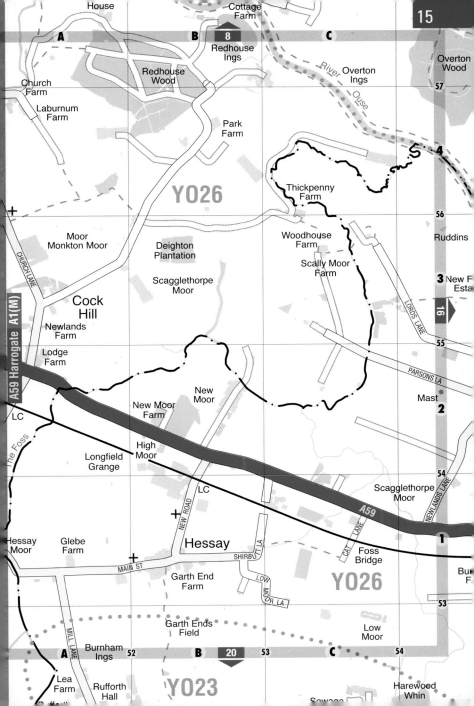

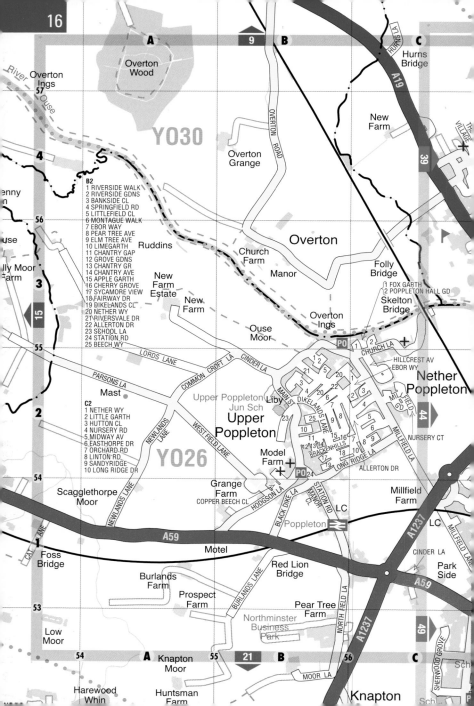

**A** · **9** · **B** · **C**

River Ouse

Overton Ings
57

Overton Wood

Hurns Bridge

A19

**YO30**

The Village

New Farm

39

4

Overton Road

Overton Grange

Overton

56

Ruddins

New Farm Estate

New Farm

Church Farm

Manor

Folly Bridge

1 FOX GARTH
2 POPPLETON HALL GD

Skelton Bridge

HILLCREST AV
EBOR WY

Nether Poppleton

3

15

**B2**
1 RIVERSIDE WALK
2 RIVERSIDE GDNS
3 BANKSIDE CL
4 SPRINGFIELD RD
5 LITTLEFIELD CL
6 MONTAGUE WALK
7 EBOR WAY
8 PEAR TREE AVE
9 ELM TREE AVE
10 LIMEGARTH
11 CHANTRY GAP
12 GROVE GDNS
13 CHANTRY GR
14 CHANTRY AVE
15 APPLE GARTH
16 CHERRY GROVE
17 SYCAMORE VIEW
18 FAIRWAY DR
19 DIKELANDS CL
20 NETHER WY
21 RIVERSVALE DR
22 ALLERTON DR
23 SCHOOL LA
24 STATION RD
25 BEECH WY

Ouse Moor

Overton Ings

P0

CHURCH LA

44

MILLFIELD GD

NURSERY CT

55

LORDS LANE

COMMON CROFT LA

CINDER LA

PARSONS LA

Mast

MAIN ST

DIKELANDS LANE

Lib¹y

Upper Poppleton Jun Sch

**C2**
1 NETHER WY
2 LITTLE GARTH
3 HUTTON CL
4 NURSERY RD
5 MIDWAY AV
6 EASTHORPE DR
7 ORCHARD RD
8 LINTON RD
9 SANDYRIDGE
10 LONG RIDGE DR

2

**Upper Poppleton**

NEWLANDS LANE

WEST FIELD LANE

**YO26**

MILLFIELD LA

LONG RIDGE LA

BRACKENHILLS

ALLERTON DR

54

Scagglethorpe Moor

Grange Farm

COPPER BEECH CL

Model Farm

P0

HODGSON LA

BLACK DIKE LA

MANOR CL

STATION RD

LC

Millfield Farm

LC

Poppleton

A1237

CINDER LA

Park Side

A59

CAT LANE

1

Foss Bridge

A59

Motel

Burlands Farm

Prospect Farm

BURLANDS LANE

Red Lion Bridge

NORTH FIELD LA

A59

53

Low Moor

Northminster Business Park

Pear Tree Farm

A1237

49

SHERWOOD GROVE

**54** · **A** Knapton Moor · **55** · **21** · **B** · **56** · **C**

Harewood Whin

Huntsman Farm

MOOR LA

Knapton

Sch

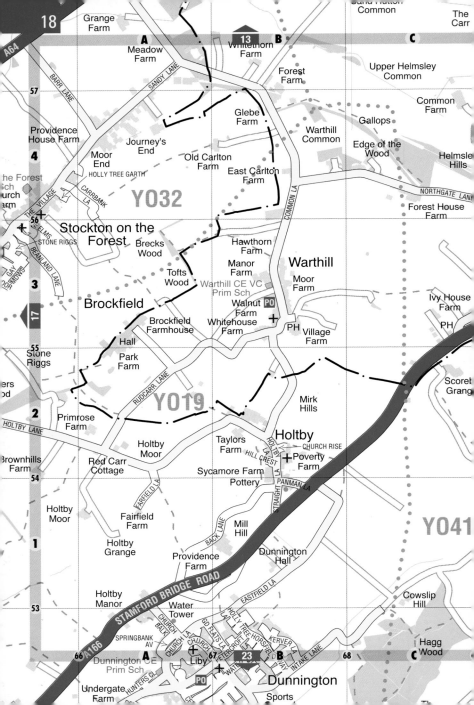

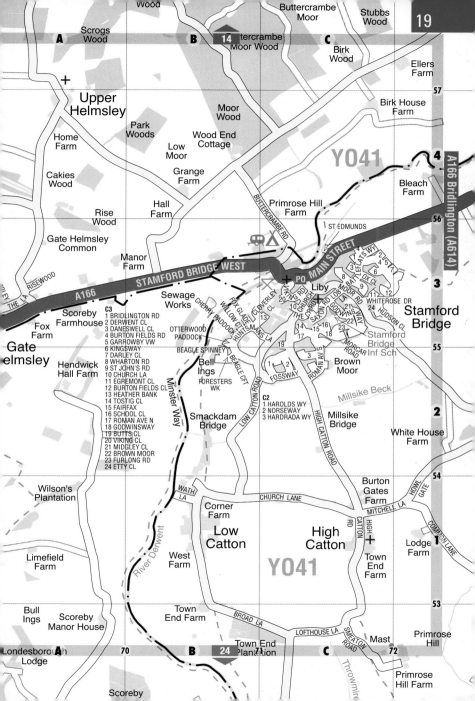

19

A  Scrogs Wood
B  14  tercrambe Moor Wood
C  Birk Wood

Wood
Buttercrambe Moor
Stubbs Wood
Ellers Farm

57

Upper Helmsley

Moor Wood

Birk House Farm

Home Farm
Park Woods
Low Moor

Wood End Cottage

Y041

4

Cakies Wood

Grange Farm

Primrose Hill Farm

Bleach Farm

A166 Bridlington (A614)

Rise Wood
Hall Farm

ST EDMUNDS

56

Gate Helmsley Common

Manor Farm

STAMFORD BRIDGE WEST

PO  MAIN STREET

3

THE LA

A166

RISEWOOD

Sewage Works

Scoreby Farmhouse

CHERRY PADDOCK

FOX GLADE

WILLOW CT

CLOVERLEY CL

VIKING RD

THE CROFT

CHURCH

SAXON RD

LOBS

GODWINS

MOOR RD

LEFLATS WY

OX CL

WHITEROSE DR

HUDSON CL

Stamford Bridge

Fox Farm

Gate elmsley

C3
1 BRIDLINGTON RD
2 DERWENT CL
3 DANESWELL CL
4 BURTON FIELDS RD
5 GARROWBY VW
6 KINGSWAY
7 DARLEY CL
8 WHARTON RD
9 ST JOHN'S RD
10 CHURCH LA
11 EGREMONT CL
12 BURTON FIELDS CL
13 HEATHER BANK
14 TOSTIG CL
15 FAIRFAX
16 SCHOOL CL
17 ROMAN AVE N
18 GODWINSWAY
19 BUTTS CL
20 VIKING CL
21 MIDGLEY CL
22 BROWN MOOR
23 FURLONG RD
24 ETTY CL

OTTERWOOD PADDOCK

BEAGLE SPINNEY

HUNTSMANS LA

BEAGLE CT

Stamford Bridge Inf Sch

55

Hendwick Hall Farm

Bell Ings

FORESTERS WK

Morcar Road

Brown Moor

Millsike Beck

Minster Way

Smackdam Bridge

LOW CATTON ROAD

FOSSWAY

ROMAN AVE N

C2
1 HAROLDS WY
2 NORSEWAY
3 HARDRADA WY

Millsike Bridge

White House Farm

2

WATH LA

Corner Farm

CHURCH LANE

HIGH CATTON ROAD

Burton Gates Farm

MITCHELL LA

HOWL GATE

54

Wilson's Plantation

West Farm

Low Catton

High Catton

HIGH CATTON RD

Town End Farm

Lodge Farm

COMMON LANE

1

Limefield Farm

River Derwent

Y041

53

Bull Ings

Scoreby Manor House

Town End Farm

BROAD LA

LOFTHOUSE LA

SMEATON ROAD

Mast

Primrose Hill

Londesborough Lodge

A  70
B  24  Town End Plantation
C  72

Primrose Hill Farm

Throwmire

Scoreby

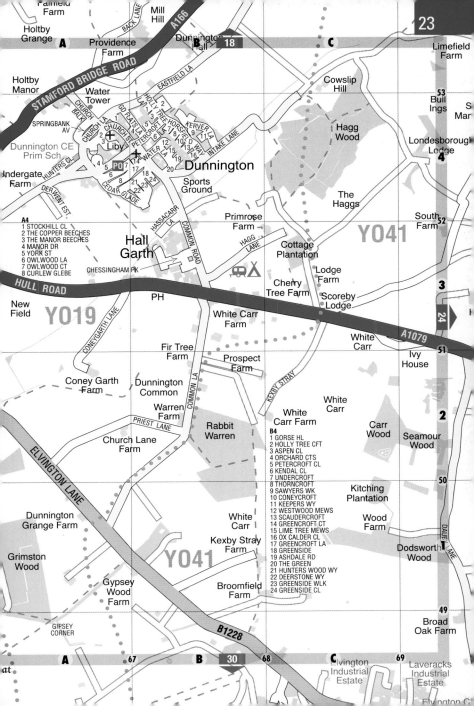

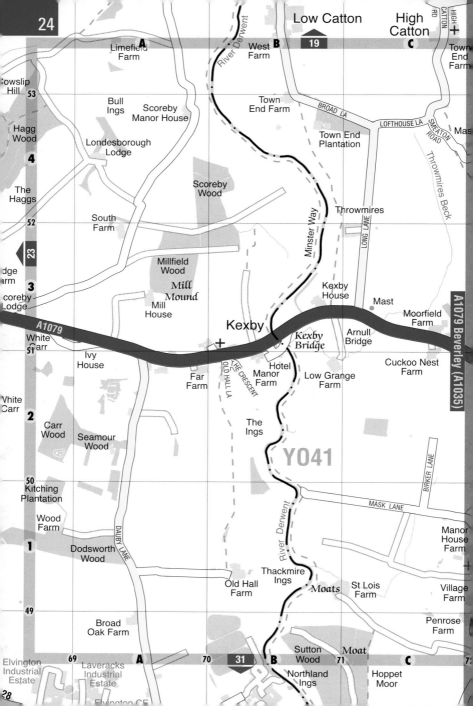

Acomb Moor

Hagg House Farm

**21**

**A**

**B**

**C**

High Moor

A1237

49

YO23

Eastfield Farm

on
on
overt

Home Farm

NORTH FIELD LANE

WEST WOOD LANE

JACKSON'S WK

skham Richard

CHURCH CL

ASKHAM BRYAN LANE

MAIN ST

**59**

**4**

ST NICHOLAS CFT

PH

Askham Bryan

SCHOOL LA

Askham Grange H.M. Prison

ASKHAM FIELDS LA

CHAPEL LANE

48

PH

BUTTACRE LA

Sewage Works

MILL LA

A1237

Cotton End

CH

Village Farmhouse

ASKHAM FIELDS

3

Eastbarrow Farm

PIKE HILL MT

TOP LANE

MERE

FLAXMA

33

Water Tower

Askham Bryan Coll

A64

COLLEGE RD

MANOR HEATH

HORSEMAN LA

13

14

11

Copmanthorpe

**25**

Askham Fields Farm

47

Buckles Inn

CAT LANE

Highfield Farm

**C2**
1 MANOR FARM CL
2 CHURCH ST
3 REYGATE GR
4 MALBYS GR
5 VICARS CL
6 DEACONS CT
7 BELLMANS CFT
8 FAIRFAX CFT
9 BEADLE GARTH
10 VAVASOUR CT
11 WILSTROP FARM RD
12 HOMEFIELD CL
13 PADDOCK CL
14 BARNFIELD WY
15 HOBSON CL
16 NALTON CL
17 LEADLEY CFT
18 SCHOOL LA
19 WESTFIELD CT
20 MOORLAND GDNS
21 ORCHARD GARTH

PO

Liby

BACK LA

MAIN ST

GILES

BRONS

Sch

Spo
Clu

STATION

DYKES LA

RD

**2**

REDHILL FIELD LA

Sewage Works

A64

Bilbrough Lodge Farm

LOW WESTFIELD ROAD

Cemy

MOOR LANE

BECK

46

REDHILL FIELD LA

Poplar Lodge Farm

Colton Haggs Farm

Hagg Wood

YO23

**C3**
1 THE LINK
2 ST NICHOLAS CR
3 ST NICHOLAS RD
4 ST NICHOLAS CL
5 LARKFIELD CL
6 LYNWOOD VW
7 RUTLAND CL
8 HORSEMAN DR
9 LYNWOOD AV
10 HORSEMAN CL
11 HORSEMAN AV
12 MILLERS CFT
13 WEAVERS CL
14 COOPERS DR
15 DRAPERS CFT
16 BARBERS DR
17 SUTOR CL
18 SADDLERS CL
19 FARRIERS CFT
20 WAGGONERS DR
21 HATTERS CL
22 POTTERS DR
23 WAINERS CL
24 FABER CL
25 CROFT FARM CL
26 GARDENERS CL
27 CORINERS DR
28 FARMERS WY
29 WHEELWRIGHT CL
30 SAWYERS CR
31 THATCHERS CFT
32 HALLCROFT LA
33 WEAVERS PARK

EARFIT LA

MOOR LANE

Moor Farm

Copmanthorpe Lodge

LS24

HAGG LANE

OLD LA

Copmanthorpe Wood

COLTON LANE

45

Colton Lodge

PH

Lady Flat Farm

Greenland Wood

Copmanthorpe Grange

**C**

PO Colton

Grange Farm

**A**

55

**B**

**33**

56

ON LANE

STREET LA

54
Lodge
Farm

Colton Brook

Brocke

ton

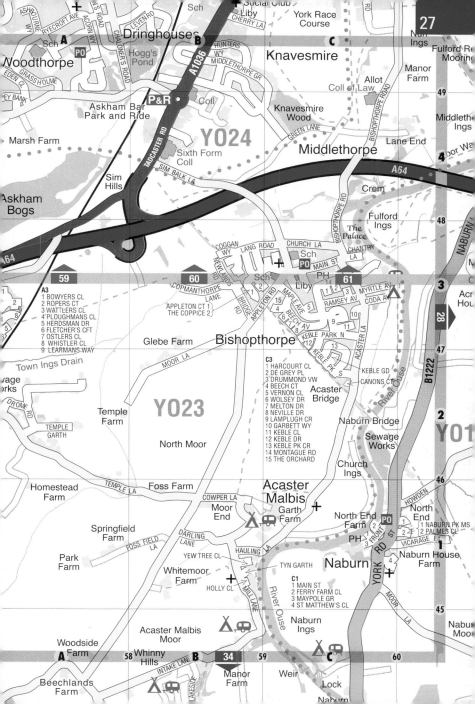

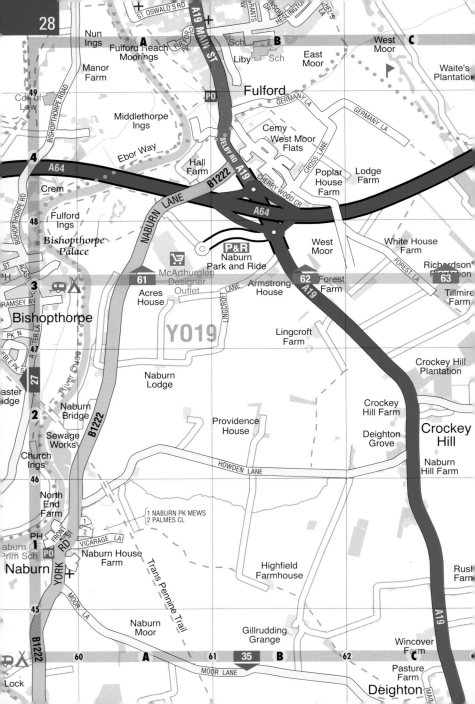

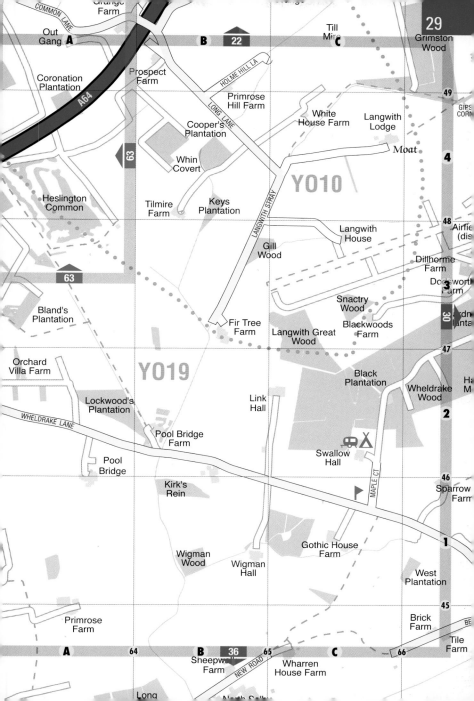

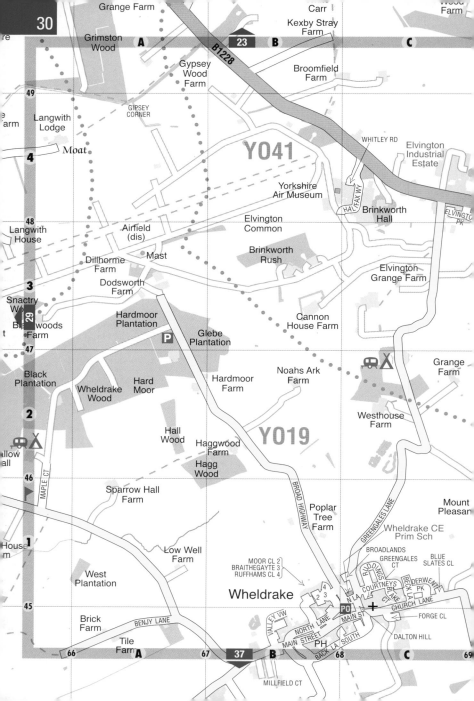

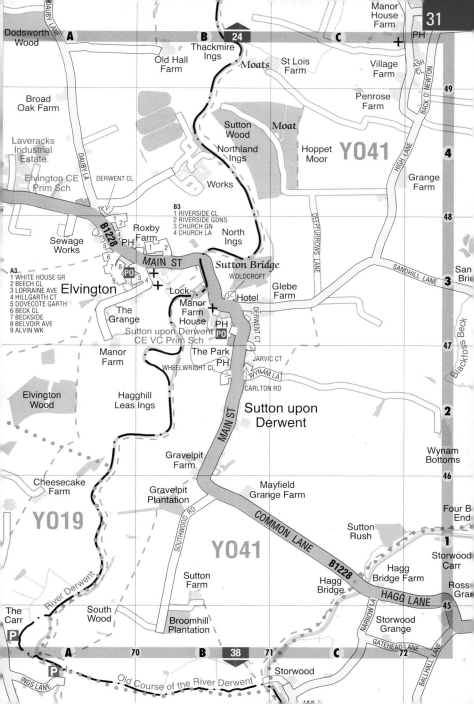

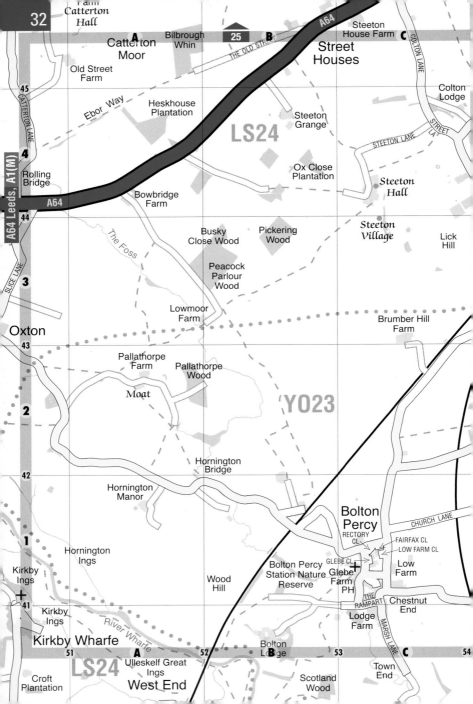

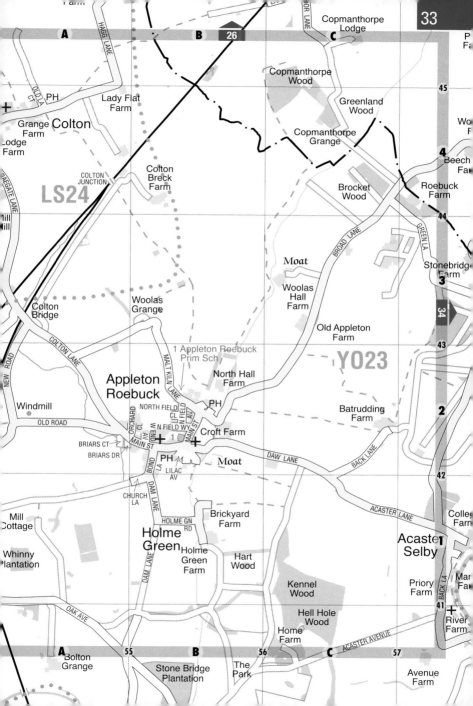

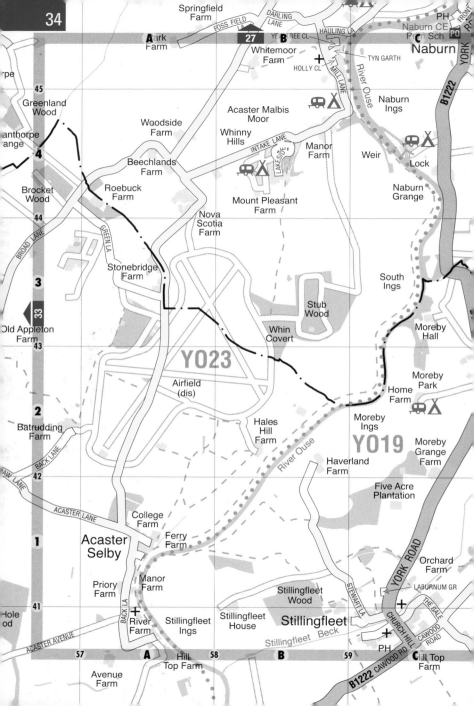

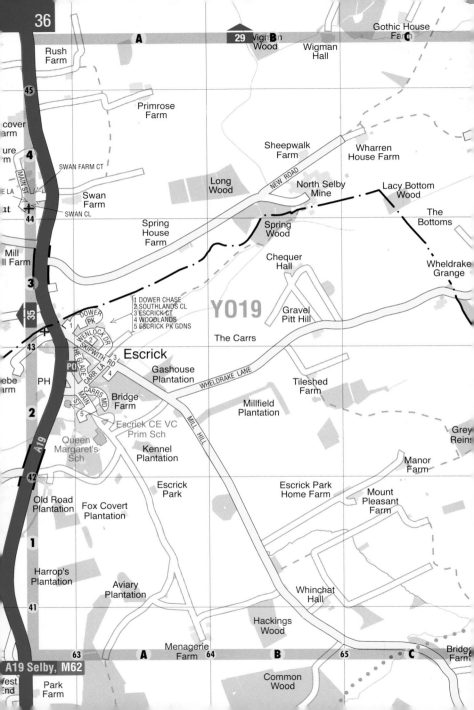

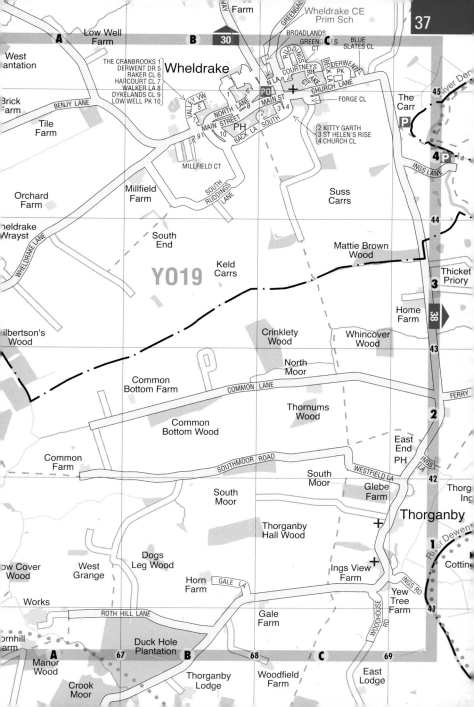

**Wheldrake**

THE CRANBROOKS 1
DERWENT DR 5
RAKER CL 6
HARCOURT CL 7
WALKER LA 8
DYKELANDS CL 9
LOW WELL PK 10

Low Well Farm

West Plantation

Brick Farm

Tile Farm

Orchard Farm

Wheldrake Wrayst

Benjy Lane

Wheldrake CE Prim Sch

GREENGA...

BROADLANDS
GREENG... CES
CT
BLUE SLATES CL

RUDDINGS LANE

COURTNEYS

BECK LA

DERWENT PK

CHURCH LANE

PO

MAIN ST

FORGE CL

VALLEY VW

NORTH LANE

MAIN STREET

PH

BACK LA SOUTH

2 KITTY GARTH
3 ST HELEN'S RISE
4 CHURCH CL

The Carr

P

45

River Derwent

INGS LANE

P

4

Millfield Farm

South Ruddings Lane

MILLFIELD CT

Suss Carrs

South End

Keld Carrs

Mattie Brown Wood

44

Thicket Priory

3

Wheldrake Lane

YO19

...ilbertson's Wood

Crinklety Wood

Whincover Wood

Home Farm

38

43

Common Bottom Farm

North Moor

COMMON LANE

Thornums Wood

FERRY

2

Common Bottom Wood

SOUTHMOOR ROAD

East End PH

INGS LA

Common Farm

South Moor

WESTFIELD LA

South Moor

Glebe Farm

Thorganby

42

Thorg Ing

Thorganby Hall Wood

Ings View Farm

River Dewen

1

Cottin

...ow Cover Wood

West Grange

Dogs Leg Wood

Horn Farm

GALE LA

Gale Farm

Yew Tree Farm

INGS RD

WOODHOUSE RD

41

Works

ROTH HILL LANE

...ornhill ...arm

Manor Wood

A

67

Duck Hole Plantation

B

Thorganby Lodge

68

Woodfield Farm

C

69

East Lodge

Crook Moor

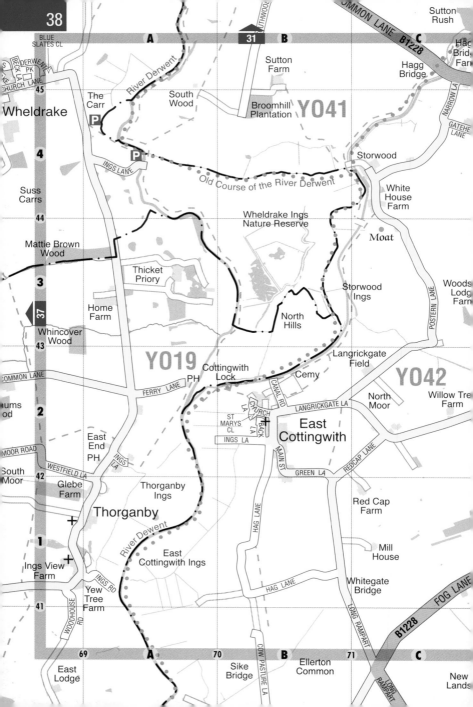

Woodside Farm

SKELTON LANE

**C**

Park Farm

**Y032**

**10**

**A**

**B**

Skelton Moor

57

**4**

MOOR LANE

**3**

**40**

**A2**
1 THE GREEN
2 THE MEADOWS
3 ORCHARD VIEW
4 THE WHEELHOUSE
5 THE DELL
6 ARTHUR PLACE

THE VILLAGE

ST GILES ROAD

Hall

**Skelton**

St Catherines

Skelton Moor

CHURCH LANE

MOORLANDS LANE

THE VILLAGE

**A19**

Skelton Prim Sch

**Y030**

**2**

BRECKSFIELD

ST GILES RD

**16**

THE VALE

PASTURE CL

PASTURE CL

1 RATCLIFFE CT
2 GREGORY CL
3 ST CATHERINES CL

PH

PE LANE

GRANGE CL

FAIRFIELDS DR

PO

SYCAMORE CL

56

**CH**

BURTREE AV

1 THE ROWMANS
2 THE BEECHES

Tees, East & North Yorkshire Ambulance Service HQ

PARK CL

**1**

Hotel

SHIPTON ROAD

River Ouse

**A**

57

Skelton Bridge

**Y026**

**B**

**44**

RAWCLIFFE LANDING
Tom Cobleighs
Riverside Farm

**C**

58

**A1237**

ST JAMES CL

HOLLYROOD RD

MOOR LANE

**A**

**B**

Plantation **C**
Farm

B1363

**10** Wigginton
Moor

WIGGINTON ROAD

Glebe
Farm

**4**

Nova Scotia
Plantation

Skelton
Moor

**57**

**YO32**

Wigginton
Lodge

MOOR LANE

Wiggington
Moor

**3**

**39**

Skelton
Moor

Skelton
Plantation

**2**

**YO30**

Moor
Plantation

Rawcliffe
Moor

**56**

Clifton
Gate Farm

Rawcliffe
Moor Farm

**1**

Clifton Moor
Retail Park

Poplar
Plantation

A1237

Clifton Moor
Sh Ctr

STIRLING RD

Clifton
Moor
Indus
Par

Clifton Moor
Retail Park

STIRLING RD

AUDAX ROAD

ATLA

**58**

**A**
ST JAMES

HOLLYROOD RD

HURRICANE WAY

MITCHELL

HANDLEYWOOD

LONGWOOD ROAD

**45**

**B**

AMY
JOHNSON

STIRLING RD

CONCORDE

**59**

AMY JOHNSON WY

BLERIOT
WY

AUDAX
CL

**C**

RING LANE

**P**

**41**

**A** **B** **C**

**10** **11**

**Haxby**

**B4**
1 PLOUGHLANDS
2 THE GREENWAY
3 FOXCROFT
4 OAK TREE CT

Villa
Farm

**4**

**57**

LC

CROMPTON
TERRACE

**Haxby
Gates**

Crompton
Farm

**3**

**42**

**C4**
1 SYCAMORE CL
2 FURNWOOD
3 SUNNYDALE
4 PINELANDS
5 MELANDER GDNS
6 ROSECOMB WAY
7 MILFORD MEWS
8 MILFORD WAY

Brecks
Farm

Wigginton
Cottage
Farm

**YO32**

A1237

Haxby Road
Farm

1 JEDWELL CL
2 SMITHIE CL
3 BEEFORTH CL
4 RYEHILL CL

Mast

PARK
TERRACE

**2**

Joseph
Rowntree
Sec Sch

**56**

PARK AVENUE

B1363

A1237

DARBIE CL 1
MALLORY CL 2
MANLEY CL 3
KENLAY CL 4
TOREMILL CL 5
MOISER CL 6

Kettlestring
Farm

LASENBY
CLOSE

LUCOMBE WY

1 2 3 4

LUCOMBE WY

1 2 3 4 5 6

PARK LODGE

HAWTHORN
PLACE

WILLOW BANK

**1**

ROWAN PL 7
ROSE TREE GR 8
CHERRY TREE AV 9
SYCAMORE AVE 10

ROWAN AVE

HAWTHORN
TERRACE

ACACIA AV

SYCAMORE
PL

Whitehall
Grange

ALMOND GR

CHESTNUT
GROVE

Clifton
Moor

**YO30**

LILAC
GR

ROWAN AVENUE

New
Earswick
Prim Sch

WILLOW BANK

POLL

**A** 60 Coppins
Farm **B** **46**

LIME TREE AVENUE

New
Earswick

PO

**61**

IVY
PLACE

ROLAND
CT

Sports
Club

Liby

STATION AVE
WESTERN

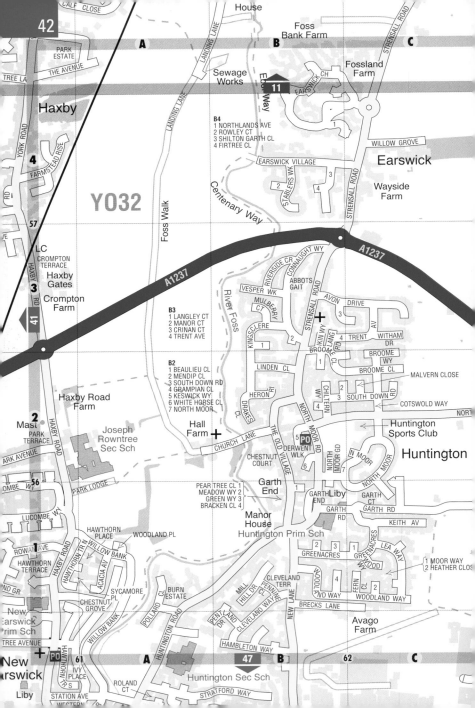

**44**

Tees, East & North Yorkshire Ambulance Service HQ

**A**

Hotel

**39**  **B**  **C**

SHIPTON ROAD

A19

*River Ouse*

**YO30**

Rawcliffe Farm

Skelton Bridge

**4**

RAWCLIFFE LANDING

*Moat*

BLENHEIM CT

MARLBOROUGH CL

Manor Farm

CHURCH LANE

Tom Cobleighs Riverside Farm

A1237

CHURCH LANE

**55**

**Nether Poppleton**

A19

HAREWOOD CL 1
KENSINGTON RD 2

1

2

ECCLES CL

MANOR LA

EVA AVENUE

FLORENCE GR

RAWCLIFFE CFT

**3**

MILLFIELD RD

NURSERY CT

**16**

SHIPTON ROAD

SHIPTON ROAD A19

INGS VILL

**YO26**

**P&R**

Sewage Works

Rawcliffe Ings

MILLFIELD LANE

**2**

BRIDGE LANE

DR

Rawcliffe Ings

**54**

Hotel

A1237

WHITE ROSE CL

Poppleton Ings

WESTMINSTER PLACE

INGS LA

WHITE ROSE WAY

GREAT NORTH WAY

GREAT NORTH WAY

Poppleton Ings

Rawcliffe Ings

**1**

KYLE WY

NIDD CL

CALDER AV

FOSS WK

BECK DR

SEVERN GN

GREAT N WAY

River Ouse

LC

MILLFIELD LANE

A1237

Acomb Ings

**9**

A1237

CINDER LA

**A**

Park Side

**57**

**49**  **B**  **C**

A59

VILLA COURT

VIEW

LETON

Works

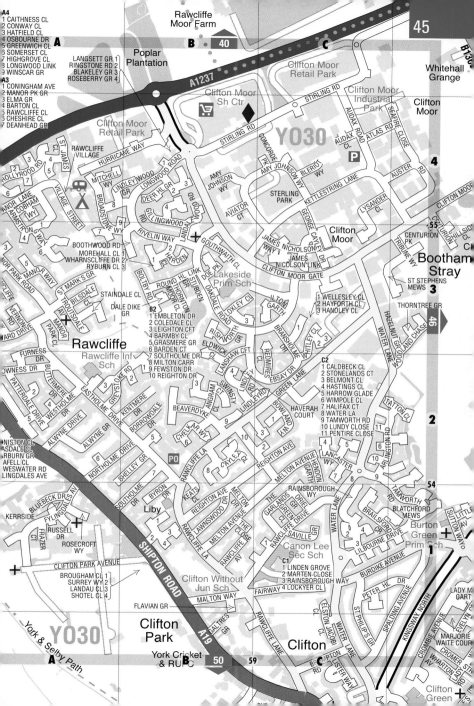

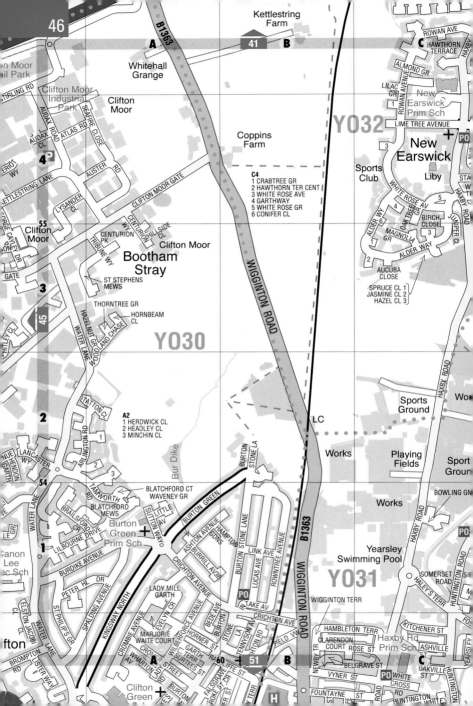

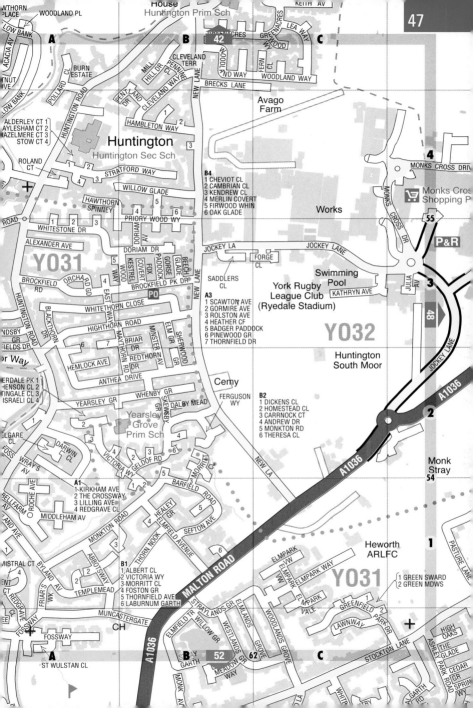

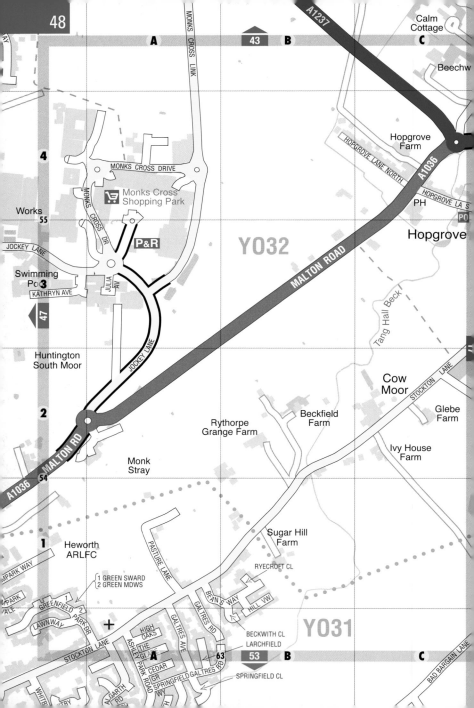

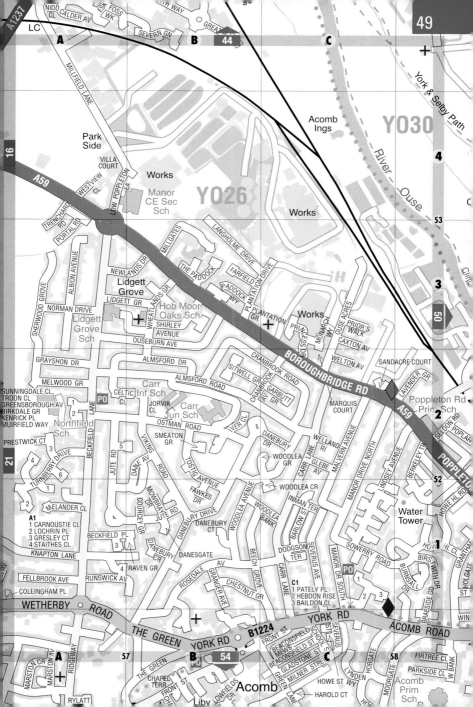

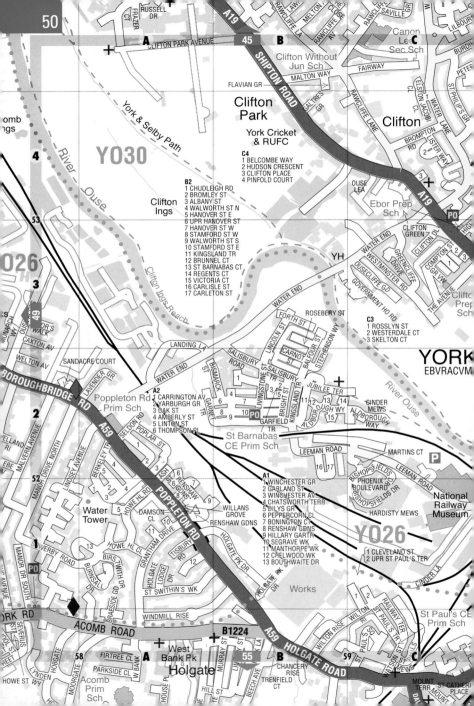

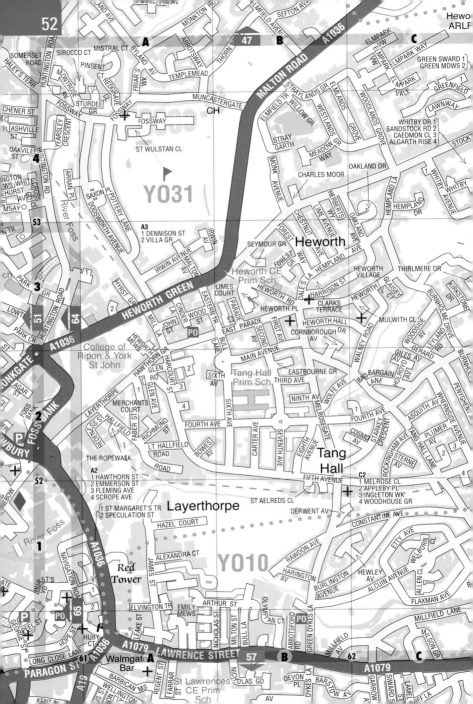

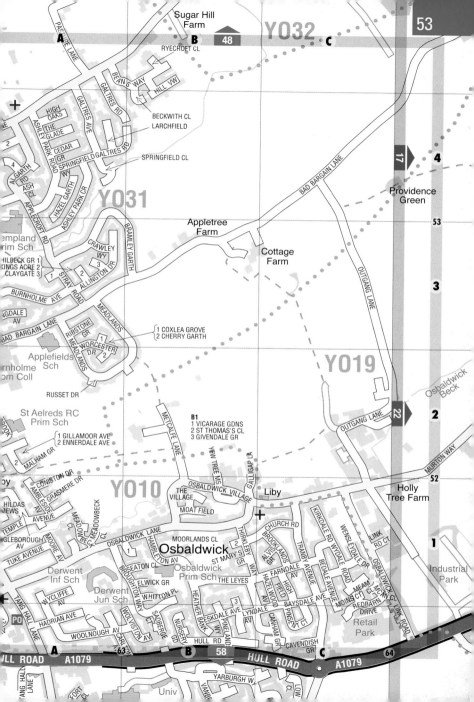

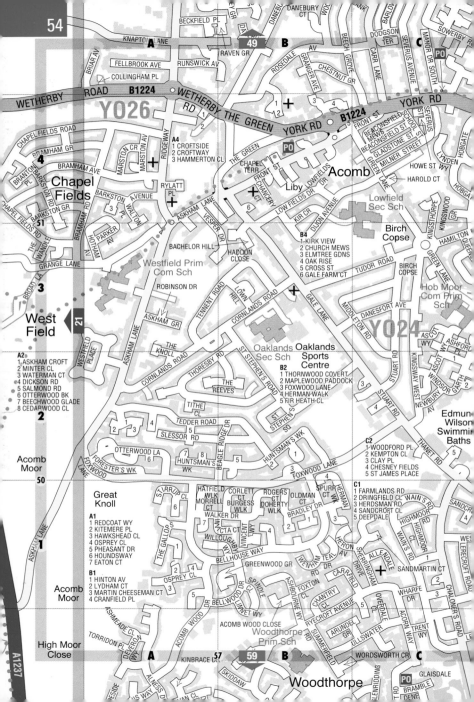

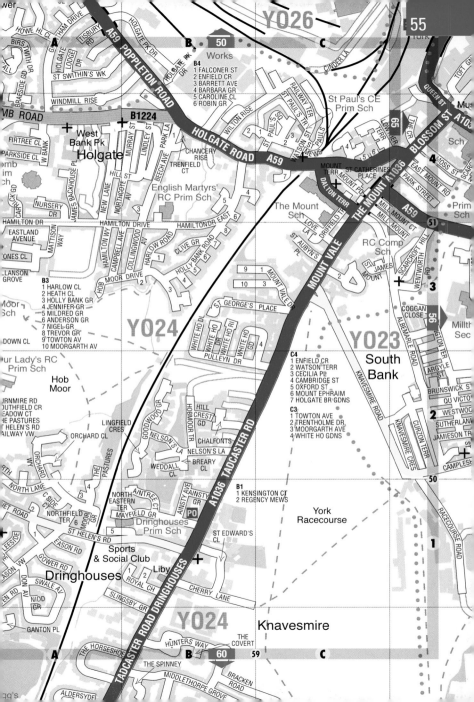

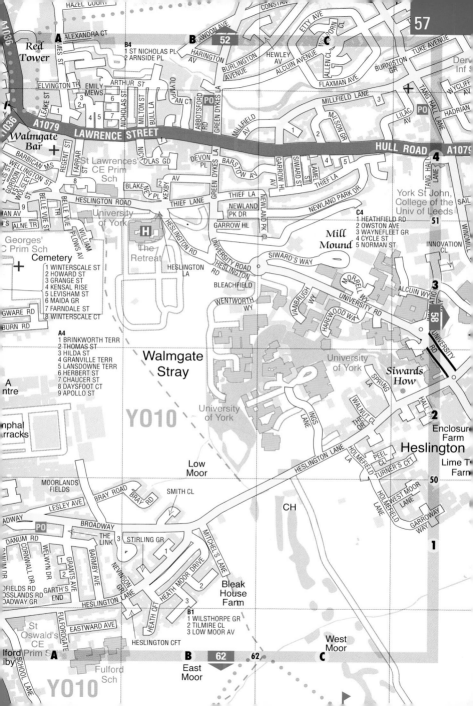

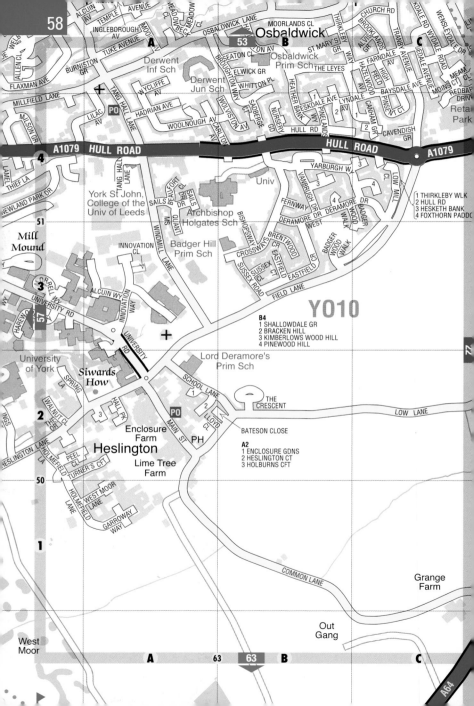

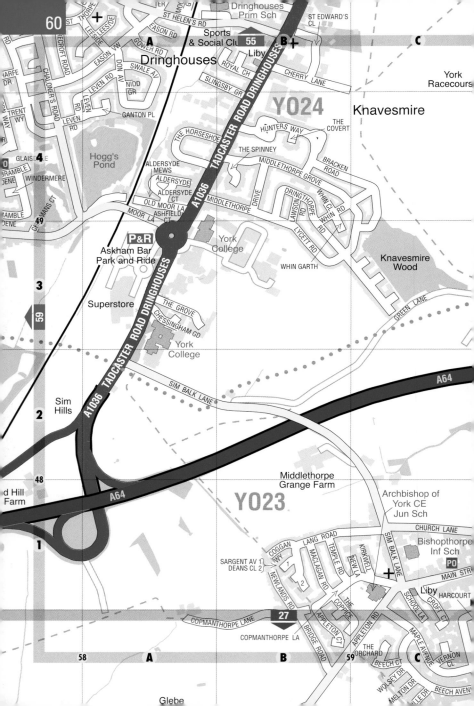

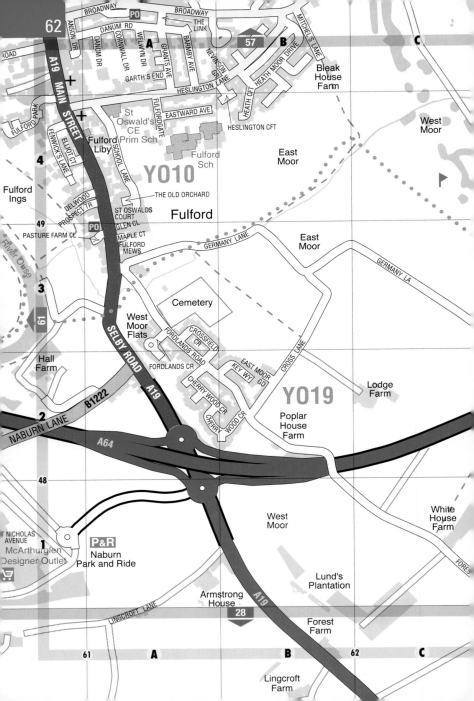

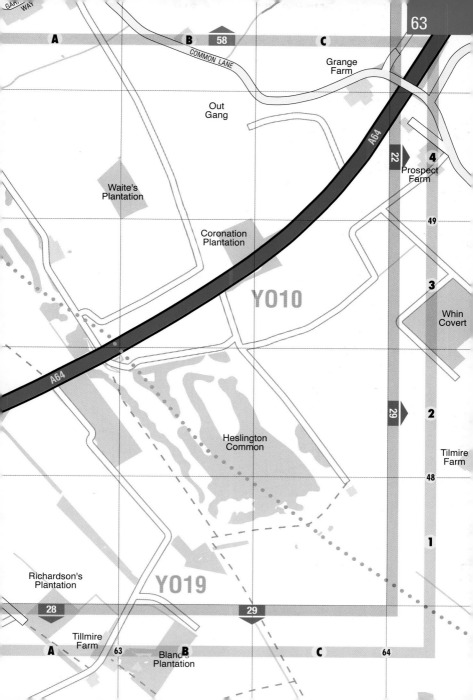

Scale: 7 inches to 1 mile
0   110 yards   220 yards
0   125 m   250 m

River Foss

51

HUNTINGTON ROAD

DALGUISE GROVE

MONKBRIDGE COURT

HEWORTH GN

A1036

FOSS BANK

A1036

Ebor Ind Est

Ebor Industrial Estate

Retail Park

The Cloisters

MONKGATE

Monk Bar & Richard III Mus

City Wall

JEWBURY   A1036

FOSS

C

GLADSTONE STREET

GROVE TERR

HAMMOND STREET

GARFIELD TERR

PARK GROVE

GROVES LANE

DUDLEY STREET

LOWTHER COURT

Pk Grove Sch

JACKSON ST

ST WILFRIDS GN

St Wilfrids RC Prim Sch

AGAR ST

MONKGATE CLOISTERS

THE CLOISTERS

Merchant Taylors Hall

MARGARET PHILLIPSON CT

TURKS HEAD CT

RAMSGATE

NEVILLE TERR

ELDON TR

AMBER ST

STANLEY ST

NELSON ST

LAMBERT CT

NEVILLE STREET

ELDON STREET

Northern Backlight Theatre

MARKHAM STREET

LOWTHER STREET

MARCH STREET

BROWNLOW STREET

PENLEY'S GROVE STREET

GROVES CT

GROVES LA

ROCKWOOD

WAVERLEY

St Maurice's RD

St Williams College

Treasurer's House

605

Clarence Gardens

MARKHAM CRESCENT

HAXBY ROAD

ST THOMAS PLACE

COLE ST

OWEN ST

LABEL

GARDEN STREET

JOHN STREET

NORTH STREET

St Williams College

MINSTER COURT

York Minster

WIGGINTON ROAD

CLARENCE STREET B1363

UNION TERRACE

BRIDGE LANE

DE GREY TERRACE

BROOK ST

BACKHOUSE ST

DE GREY STREET

Robin Hood Tower

LORD MAYOR'S WALK

YORK
EBVRACVM

Minster Liby & Archives

City Wall

THE MINSTER YARD

MINSTER YARD

Minster Gate

The Minster School

B

York District H

York District Hospital

H

Bootham Park

BOOTHAM PARK COURT

Coach Park P

Gate

GROSVENOR ROAD

GROSVENOR TERRACE

BOOTHAM TERRACE

CLAREMONT TERR

PORTLAND STREET

BOOTHAM ROW

PERCY ST

GILLYGATE

A1036

MONKBAR

Bootham Bar

Purey Cust Nuffield

ST LEONARD'S PL   A1036

Theatre Royal

i

Assembly

BLAKE

York City Football Club

GROSVENOR HOUSE

Bootham Sch

ST OLAVES ROAD

A19   BOOTHAM

ST MARY'S LANE

ALMA... LA

St Mary's Tower

York Art Gallery

St Mary's Abbey

King's Manor

University of York

EXHIBITION SQ

Central Library

Observatory

MARYGATE

Yorkshire Museum

Museum Gardens

A

NORTH GRANGE CT

BURTON STONE LANE

AVENUE RD

DE GREY TERR

PETERSWAY

ST PETERS COURT

ST PETERS GROVE

QUEEN ANNE'S ROAD

NORTH PARADE

SYCAMORE PL

ST MARY'S

ST MARY'S TERR

MARYGATE LANE

FREDERIC ST

HETHERTON

BOOTHAM TERRACE

LONGFIELD TERRACE

MARYGATE TERR

ESPLANADE

EARLSBOROUGH TERR

SYCAMORE TERRACE

ALMERY TER

CLIFTON   A19

St Peter's Sch

Clifton Prep Sch

YO30

Playing Field

St Olave's School

Playing Fields

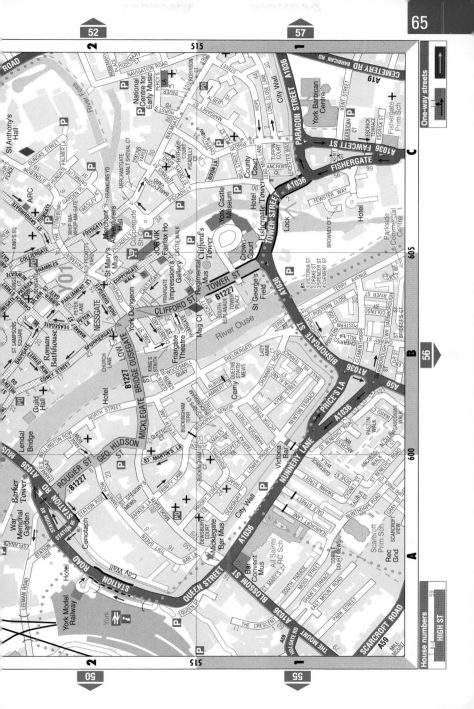

# Index

Street names are listed alphabetically and show the locality, the Postcode District, the page number and a reference to the square in which the name falls on the map page

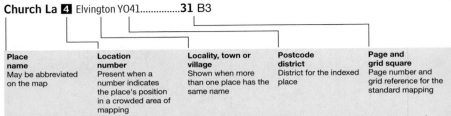

**Church La** Elvington YO41 ............... **31** B3

| **Place name** | **Location number** | **Locality, town or village** | **Postcode district** | **Page and grid square** |
|---|---|---|---|---|
| May be abbreviated on the map | Present when a number indicates the place's position in a crowded area of mapping | Shown when more than one place has the same name | District for the indexed place | Page number and grid reference for the standard mapping |

**Public and commercial buildings** are highlighted in magenta. **Places of interest** are highlighted in blue with a star*
**Cities, towns and villages** are listed in CAPITAL LETTERS

## Abbreviations used in the index

| Acad | **Academy** | Comm | **Common** | Gd | **Ground** | L | **Leisure** | Prom | **Promenade** |
|---|---|---|---|---|---|---|---|---|---|
| App | **Approach** | Cott | **Cottage** | Gdn | **Garden** | La | **Lane** | Rd | **Road** |
| Arc | **Arcade** | Cres | **Crescent** | Gn | **Green** | Liby | **Library** | Recn | **Recreation** |
| Ave | **Avenue** | Cswy | **Causeway** | Gr | **Grove** | Mdw | **Meadow** | Ret | **Retail** |
| Bglw | **Bungalow** | Ct | **Court** | H | **Hall** | Meml | **Memorial** | Sh | **Shopping** |
| Bldg | **Building** | Ctr | **Centre** | Ho | **House** | Mkt | **Market** | Sq | **Square** |
| Bsns, Bus | **Business** | Ctry | **Country** | Hospl | **Hospital** | Mus | **Museum** | St | **Street** |
| Bvd | **Boulevard** | Cty | **County** | HQ | **Headquarters** | Orch | **Orchard** | Sta | **Station** |
| Cath | **Cathedral** | Dr | **Drive** | Hts | **Heights** | Pal | **Palace** | Terr | **Terrace** |
| Cir | **Circus** | Dro | **Drove** | Ind | **Industrial** | Par | **Parade** | TH | **Town Hall** |
| Cl | **Close** | Ed | **Education** | Inst | **Institute** | Pas | **Passage** | Univ | **University** |
| Cnr | **Corner** | Emb | **Embankment** | Int | **International** | Pk | **Park** | Wk, Wlk | **Walk** |
| Coll | **College** | Est | **Estate** | Intc | **Interchange** | Pl | **Place** | Wr | **Water** |
| Com | **Community** | Ex | **Exhibition** | Junc | **Junction** | Prec | **Precinct** | Yd | **Yard** |

## Index of towns, villages, streets, hospitals, industrial estates, railway stations, shopping centres, universities and places of interest

### Abb – Bea

### A

Abbey St YO30 ..... 50 C4
Abbotsford Rd YO10 . 57 B4
Abbots Gait YO32 .... 42 B3
Abbot St YO31 ........ 64 C4
Abbotsway YO31 ..... 47 A1
Abelton Gr 33 YO32.. 11 A2
Acacia Ave YO32 .... 42 A1
Acacia Gr 38 YO32.. 11 A2
Acaster La
 Acaster Malbis YO23 . 27 C2
 Acaster Selby YO23 .. 33 C1
ACASTER MALBIS .. 27 C1
ACASTER SELBY .... 34 A1
ACOMB .................. 54 B4
Acomb Prim Sch
 YO24................... 55 A4
Acomb Rd YO24 ...... 54 C4
Acomb Wood Cl
 YO24................... 59 B4
Acomb Wood Dr
 YO24................... 59 A4
Acorn Way YO24 ..... 59 C4
Adelaide St 3 YO23. 56 A3
Adlington Cl 3 YO32 11 C4
Agar St YO31 .......... 64 C3
Ainsty Ave YO24 ..... 55 B1
Ainsty Gr YO24 ....... 55 B1
Aintree Ct YO24 ...... 55 B1
Albany St 3 YO26 ... 56 B2
Albemarle Rd YO23.. 56 A3
Albert Cl 1 YO32.... 4 B1
Albert St YO10 ....... 65 C1
Albion Ave YO26..... 49 A3
Albion St YO11 ....... 65 B1
Alcelina Ct YO23 .... 65 B1
Alcuin Ave YO10..... 52 C1

Alcuin Way YO10 .... 58 A3
Aldborough Way
 YO30..................... 
 YO26................... 50 B2
Alderley Ct YO24 .... 47 A4
Aldersyde YO24 ...... 60 A4
Aldersyde Ct YO24... 60 A4
Aldersyde Mews
 YO24................... 60 A4
Alder Way YO32 ..... 46 C3
Aldreth Gr YO23 ..... 56 B3
Aldwark YO1 .......... 64 C3
Alexander Ave YO31 47 A3
Alexandra Ct YO10 .. 52 A1
Alexandra Rd YO12.. 11 C3
Algarth Rd YO31..... 53 A4
Algarth Rise YO31 .. 53 A4
Allanson Gr YO24.... 55 A3
Allan St 2 YO30..... 51 B4
Allen Cl YO10 ......... 52 C1
Allendale YO24 ...... 54 C1
Allerton Dr 22 YO26. 16 B2
Allington Dr YO31 ... 27 B3
Allotments La YO61 .. 3 B4
All Saints' RC Sch
 YO24................... 
Alma Gr YO10 ........ 56 C3
Alma Terr YO10...... 56 C3
Almery Terr YO30.... 64 A3
Almond Gr YO32 ..... 41 C1
Almsford Dr YO26 ... 49 B2
Almsford Rd YO26... 49 B2
Alness Dr YO24 ...... 59 A4
Alne Terr YO10 ....... 57 A3
Alvin Wlk 9 YO41... 31 A3
Alvis Gr YO10 ........ 53 C1
Alwyne Dr YO30 ..... 45 A2
Alwyne Gr YO30 ..... 45 A2
Amber Ct YO01....... 64 A4
Amberly St 4 YO26 . 50 A2
Amber St YO01 ....... 64 A4
Ambler's La YO30 .... 9 B4
Ambleside Ave YO10. 53 A1
Ambrose St YO10.... 56 C2

Amy Johnson Way
 YO30..................... 45 C4
Ancress Wlk YO23 .. 65 A1
Ancroft Cl YO1 ....... 65 C1
Anderson Gr 6 YO24 55 B3
Andrew Dr 4 YO32.. 47 B2
ANGRAM ............... 25 B4
Angram Cl YO30..... 45 B2
Angram La YO61 ..... 2 A4
Annan Cl YO24 ...... 59 B3
Anne St YO23 ........ 56 B3
Anson Dr YO10 ...... 56 C1
Anthea Dr YO31 ..... 47 A2
Apollo St 9 YO10 ... 57 A4
Appleby Glade YO32 41 C4
Appleby Pl 2 YO31.. 52 C2
Applecroft Rd YO31 . 53 A4
Applefields Sch
 YO31................... 53 A2
Apple Garth 19 YO26 16 B2
Appleton Ct YO23 ... 27 B3
Appleton Rd YO23... 27 B3
APPLETON ROEBUCK
 ........................... 33 B2
Appleton Roebuck Prim
 Sch 1 YO23....... 33 B2
ARC* YO1 ............... 58 C4
Archbishop Holgate's
 Sch YO10 ........... 58 A4
Archbishop of York CE
 Jun Sch YO23 .... 60 C1
Arenhall Cl 10 YO32 11 A1
Argyle St YO23 ....... 56 A2
Arlington Rd YO30... 45 C2
Armstrong Way
 YO32..................... 45 A4
Arnside Pl 2 YO10.. 57 B4
Arran Pl YO31........ 51 C4
Arthur Pl 6 YO30 ... 39 A2
Arthur St YO10 ...... 52 A1
Arundel Gr YO24 .... 59 B4
Ascot Rd YO32 ...... 10 C2
Ascot Way YO24 .... 54 C2

Ashbourne Way
 YO24..................... 54 B1
Ash Cl YO31........... 53 A4
Ashdale Rd 10 YO19 . 23 B4
Ashfield Ct YO24 .... 60 A4
Ashford Pl YO24..... 54 C3
Ash La 8 YO32....... 11 A2
Ashley Pk Cres YO31 53 A3
Ashley Pk Rd YO31 . 53 A4
Ashmeade Cl YO24 . 54 A1
Ash St YO26........... 50 A1
Ashton Ave YO30..... 46 A1
Ashville St YO31..... 51 C4
Ashwood Glade YO32 41 B3
Askham Bog Nature
 Reserve* YO23 .... 59 B2
ASKHAM BRYAN .... 26 B4
Askham Bryan Coll
 YO23................... 26 B3
Askham Bryan La
 YO23................... 26 B4
Askham Croft 1
 YO24................... 54 A2
Askham Fields La
 YO23................... 26 B3
Askham Gr YO24 .... 54 A3
Askham La
 Askham Bryan YO24.. 21 C1
 York YO24............. 54 A2
ASKHAM RICHARD . 25 C4
Aspen Cl 3 YO19.... 23 B4
Asquith Ave YO31 ... 47 A2
Atcherley Cl YO10... 56 C1
Atlas Rd YO30........ 45 C4
Aucuba Cl YO32...... 46 C3
Audax Cl YO30 ...... 45 C4
Audax Rd YO30...... 45 C4
Auster Rd YO30 ..... 46 A4
Avenue Rd YO30..... 64 A4
Avenue Terr YO30... 64 A4
Avenue The
 3 Haxby YO23..... 11 A2
 Rufforth YO23....... 20 B3

Avenue The continued
 York YO30............. 50 C3
Aviator Ct YO30 ..... 45 B4
Avon Dr YO32 ........ 42 B3
Aylesham Ct YO32... 47 A4

### B

Bachelor Hill YO24 .. 54 B3
Backhouse St YO31.. 64 B4
Back La
 Appleton Roebuck
 YO23................... 33 C2
 Bilbrough YO23...... 25 C2
 Copmanthorpe YO23 . 26 C2
 Cottingwith YO42.... 38 B2
 Flaxton YO60 ......... 7 B2
 11 Haxby YO32..... 10 C2
 Holtby YO19 ......... 18 A1
 Newton-on-Ouse YO30. 8 A3
 York YO26.............. 21 C4
 York La S YO19 ..... 37 B4
Back W View 2
 YO30..................... 51 A4
Bad Bargain La YO31 52 C2
Badger Hill Prim Sch
 YO10................... 58 A3
Badger Paddock 5
 YO31..................... 47 A3
Badger Wood Wlk
 YO10................... 58 C4
Baildon Cl 3 YO26.. 49 C1
Baile Hill Terr YO1... 65 B1
Baker St YO30........ 51 B4
Balfour St YO26 ..... 21 C4
Balfour Way YO32 ... 11 C3
Balmoral Terr 5
 YO23..................... 56 A2
Bankside Cl 3 YO26. 16 B2
Bannisdale 6 YO24 . 59 B4
Barbara Gr 4 YO24 . 55 B4

### Abb – Bea

Barbers Dr
 16 Copmanthorpe
 YO23................... 26 C3
 Copmanthorpe YO23 . 59 A1
Barbican Ct YO10.... 65 C1
Barbican Mews YO10 57 A4
Barbican Rd YO10 ... 65 C1
Bar Convent Mus*
 YO24................... 65 A1
Barden Ct 6 YO30 .. 45 B2
Barfield Rd YO31 .... 47 B1
Barker La YO1........ 65 A2
Barkston Ave
 7 York YO26......... 21 C3
 York YO26............. 54 A4
Barkston Cl 3 YO26. 21 C3
Barkston Gr 6 YO26 21 C3
Barkston Rd YO26 ... 21 C3
Bar La YO1 ............ 65 A2
Barleycorn Yd YO1 .. 65 C2
Barley Hall* YO1..... 64 B3
Barley Rise YO32 .... 11 C3
Barley View 10 YO32 11 A1
Barlow St YO26....... 49 C1
Barmby Ave YO10 ... 57 A3
Barmby Cl 4 YO30 .. 45 B2
Barney La YO60...... 7 B2
Barnfield Way 14
 YO23..................... 26 C2
Barons Cres YO23 ... 26 C2
Barrett Ave 3 YO24 . 55 B4
Barr La YO32 ......... 12 C1
Barstow Ave YO10 .. 57 B4
Bartle Garth YO1 .... 64 C3
Barton Cl 4 YO31 ... 45 A3
Bateson Cl YO31..... 51 C4
Battleflats Way YO41 19 C3
Baysdale Ave YO10 . 58 C4
Beaconsfield Mews
 YO24..................... 54 C4
Beaconsfield St
 YO24..................... 54 C4

Beadle Garth 9 YO23 26 C2
Beagle Croft YO41 19 B2
Beagle Ridge Dr YO24 54 B2
Beagle Spinney YO41 19 B2
Beanland La YO32 17 C3
Bean's Way YO31 48 A1
Beaufort Cl YO10 58 A4
Beaulieu Cl 1 YO32 42 B2
Beaverdyke YO30 45 B2
Beck Cl 6 YO41 31 A3
Beckfield La YO26 49 A2
Beckfield Pl YO26 49 A1
Beck La YO19 30 C1
Becks Cl 18 YO32 11 A1
Beckside 7 YO41 31 A3
Beckwith Cl YO31 53 B4
Bedale Ave YO10 53 C1
Bede Ave YO30 51 A4
Bedern YO1 64 C3
Beech Ave
Bishopthorpe YO23 27 C3
York YO24 55 B4
Beech Cl 2 YO41 31 A3
Beech Ct 4 YO23 27 C3
Beeches The YO30 39 B1
Beechfield YO30 8 A3
Beech Glade YO31 47 B3
Beech Gr YO26 49 B1
Beech Pl 5 YO32 11 C3
Beech Way 25 YO26 16 B2
Beechwood Glade 7 YO24 54 A2
Beeforth Cl YO32 41 C2
Belcombe Way 1 YO30 50 C4
Belgrave St YO31 51 B4
Bell Cl 14 YO32 11 A1
Belle Vue St YO10 57 A4
Belle Vue Terr YO10 57 A4
Bellfarm Ave YO31 47 A4
Bellground La YO30 8 C1
Bell Hall★ YO19 35 A3
Bellhouse Way YO24 54 A1
Bellmans Croft 7 YO23 26 C2
Bellwood Dr YO24 54 A1
Belmont Cl 3 YO30 45 C2
Belvoir Ave 8 YO41 31 A3
Beningborough Hall & Gdns★ YO30 8 A2
BENINGBROUGH 8 C1
Beningbrough La YO30 8 C2
Benjy La YO19 37 A4
Beresford Terr YO23 56 B2
Berkeley Terr YO26 50 A2
Beverley Balk YO41 19 A3
Bewlay St YO23 56 B3
BILBROUGH 25 C2
Bilsdale Cl YO30 45 A3
Birch Cl YO32 46 C4
Birch Copse YO24 54 C3
Birch La 13 YO32 11 A2
Birkdale Gr 4 YO26 49 A2
Birker La YO41 24 C1
Birstwith Dr YO26 50 A1
Bishopgate St YO23 65 B1
Bishophill Jun YO1 65 A1
Bishophill Senior YO1 65 B1
Bishops Ct YO1 65 B1
Bishopsfields Dr YO26 50 C2
Bishopsway YO10 58 B4
BISHOPTHORPE 27 B3
Bishopthorpe Inf Sch YO23 60 C1
Bishopthorpe Pal★ YO23 61 A1
Bishopthorpe Rd YO23 61 A2
Bismarck St YO26 50 A2
Black Dike La YO26 16 B1
Blacklee Cl 4 YO32 6 A1
Blackthorn Dr YO31 47 A3
Blake Ct YO19 30 C1
Blakeley Gr YO30 45 B4
Blakeney Pl YO10 57 B4
Blake St YO1 64 B3
Bland La YO26 21 C3
Blatchford YO30 46 A1
Blatchford Mews YO30 46 A1
Bleachfield YO10 57 B3
Blenheim Ct YO30 44 C4
Bleriot Way YO30 45 C4
Blossom St YO24 65 A1
Bluebeck Dr YO30 45 A1
Blue Bridge La YO10 56 C3
Blue Slates Cl YO19 30 C1
Bog La YO24 59 A3
Boltby Rd YO30 45 B3
BOLTON PERCY 32 C1
Bolton Percy Station Nature Reserve★ YO23 32 B1
Bond La YO23 33 B2
Bonington Ct 7 YO26 50 A1
Bootham YO30 64 A3
Bootham Bar★ YO31 64 B3
Bootham Cres YO30 64 A4
Bootham Pk Ct YO31 64 B4
Bootham Pk Hospl YO31 64 B4
Bootham Row YO31 64 B3
Bootham Sch YO31 64 A3
Bootham Sq YO31 64 B3
BOOTHAM STRAY 47 B4
Bootham Terr YO30 64 A3
Boothwood Rd YO30 45 A3
Bore Tree Baulk YO19 22 C3
Boroughbridge Rd YO26 49 C2
Borrowdale Dr YO30 45 B2
BOSSALL 14 C4
Bouthwaite Dr 13 YO26 50 A1
Bowes Ave YO31 52 A2
Bowland Way YO30 45 C2
Bowling Gn Ct YO31 46 C1
Bowling Gn La YO31 64 C4
Bowness Dr YO30 45 A2
Bowyers Cl 1 YO23 27 A3
Bracken Cl YO32 42 B1
Bracken Hill 2 YO10 58 B4
Brackenhills YO26 16 B2
Bracken Rd YO24 60 B4
Bradley Cres YO23 20 C3
Bradley Dr YO24 54 B1
Bradley La YO23 20 B2
Braegate La LS24 33 A4
Braeside Gdns YO24 55 A4
Brailsford Cres YO30 45 C1
Braithegayte YO19 30 B1
Bramble Dene YO24 59 C4
Bramham Ave YO26 21 C3
Bramham Gr 4 YO26 21 C3
Bramham Rd YO26 21 C2
Bramley Garth YO31 53 A3
Brandon Gr YO32 17 B3
Brandsby Gr YO31 47 A3
Bransholme Dr YO30 45 C3
Branton Pl 5 YO26 21 C3
Bravener Ct YO30 8 A3
Bray Rd YO10 57 B1
Breary Cl YO24 55 B2
Brecksfield YO30 39 B2
Brecks La
Strensall YO32 12 A4
York YO32 42 B1
Brentwood Cres YO10 58 B3
Briar Ave YO26 49 A1
Briar Dr YO31 47 B3
Briars Ct YO23 33 A2
Briars Dr YO23 33 A2
Bridge Cl YO32 41 B4
Bridge La YO30 64 B4
Bridge Rd YO23 27 B3
Bridge St YO1 65 B2
Bridle Way 1 YO26 21 C3
Bridlington Rd 1 YO41 19 C3
Briergate YO32 41 B4
Briggs St YO31 51 B4
Bright St YO26 50 B2
Brinkworth Terr 1 YO10 57 A4
Broad Acres YO32 41 B4
Broad Highway YO19 30 B1
Broad La
Appleton Roebuck YO23 33 C3
Catton YO41 24 B4
Rufforth YO23 21 C2
Broadlands YO19 30 C1
Broad Oak YO61 4 C1
Broad Oak La 18 YO32 11 A2
Broadstone Way YO30 45 A4
Broadway YO10 57 A1
Broadway Gr 3 YO10 57 A1
Broadway W YO10 56 C1
BROCKFIELD 18 A3
Brockfield Pk Dr YO31 47 B3
Brockfield Rd YO31 47 A3
Bromley St 2 YO26 50 B2
Brompton Rd YO30 50 C4
Brooklands YO10 53 C1
Brook St YO31 64 B4
Broome Cl YO32 42 B2
Broome Way YO32 42 C2
Brougham Cl YO30 45 B1
Broughton Way YO10 53 A1
Browney Croft YO10 65 C1
Brownlow St YO31 64 C4
Brown Moor 22 YO41 19 C3
Brownmoor La
Huby YO61 3 C3
Sutton-on-the-Forest YO61 4 A1
Brunel Ct 12 YO26 50 B2
Brunswick Cl 2 YO32 6 B1
Brunswick St YO23 56 A2
Buckingham Ct YO1 65 A1
Buckingham St YO1 65 B1
Buckingham Terr YO1 65 B2
Bull La Huby YO61 10 A4
York YO10 57 B4
Bull Moor La YO60 7 C1
Burdike Ave YO30 45 C1
Burgess Wlk YO24 54 B1
Burlands La YO26 21 B4
Burlington Ave YO10 52 B1
Burn Est YO32 42 A1
Burnholme Ave YO31 53 A3
Burnholme Com Coll YO31 52 C2
Burnholme Dr YO31 52 C3
Burnholme Gr YO31 52 C2
Burniston Gr YO10 52 C1
Burnsall Dr YO26 50 A1
Burns Ct YO24 59 A4
Burrill Ave YO30 46 A1
Burrill Dr 13 YO32 10 C2
Burton Ave YO30 51 A4
Burton Ct YO30 64 A4
Burton Fields Cl 12 YO41 19 C3
Burton Fields Rd 4 YO41 19 C3
Burton Gn YO30 46 A1
Burton Gn Prim Sch YO30 46 A1
Burton Stone La YO30 64 A4
Burtree Ave YO30 39 A1
Butcher Terr YO23 56 B2
Buttacre La YO23 25 C3
Buttercrambe Rd YO41 19 B4
Buttermere Dr YO30 45 A2
Butters Cl 20 YO32 10 C2
Butt Hill 22 YO32 10 C2
Butts Cl 19 YO41 19 C3
Byland Ave YO31 47 A1
Byron Dr YO30 45 B1

## C

Caedmon Cl YO31 52 C4
Cairnborrow 4 YO24 59 A4
Caithness Cl 1 YO30 45 A4
Caldbeck Cl 1 YO30 45 C2
Calder Ave YO26 44 A1
Calf Cl YO32 11 A1
Calvert Cl YO32 41 B4
Cambrian Cl 2 YO32 47 B4
Cambridge St 4 YO24 55 C4
Cameron Gr YO23 56 B2
Campbell Ave YO24 55 A3
Campleshon Rd YO23 56 A2
Canal Rd YO42 38 B2
Canham Gr YO10 58 C4
Canon Lee Sec Sch YO30 45 C1
Canons Ct YO23 27 C2
Canterbury Cl 9 YO32 10 C2
Carey St YO10 56 C2
Carleton St 17 YO26 50 B2
Carlisle St 16 YO26 50 B2
Carl St YO23 56 B3
Carlton Ave YO10 58 A4
Carlton Rd YO41 31 B2
Carmelite St YO1 65 C2
Carmires Ave YO32 11 B2
Carnot St YO26 50 B2
Carnoustie Cl 1 YO26 49 A1
Caroline Cl 5 YO24 55 B4
Carrbank La YO32 18 A4
Carrfield YO24 54 B1
Carrick Gdns YO24 55 A4
Carr Inf Sch YO26 49 B2
Carrington Ave 1 YO26 50 A2
Carr Jun Sch YO26 49 B2
Carr La Escrick YO19 36 A2
Sutton-on-the-Forest YO61 4 C3
York YO26 49 C2
Carrnock Ct 3 YO32 47 B2
Carron Cres YO24 59 A4
Carrs Mdw YO19 36 A2
Carter Ave YO31 52 B2
Castle Cl 1 YO32 10 C2
Castlegate YO1 65 B2
Castle Wlk YO1 65 C2
Cat La YO23 25 C2
CATTERTON 25 A1
Cavendish Gr YO10 58 C4
Caxton Ave YO26 49 C3
Cayley Cl YO30 45 B2
Cecilia Pl 3 YO24 55 C4
Cedar Glade YO19 23 A4
Cedar Gr YO31 53 A4
Cedarwood Cl 8 YO24 54 A2
Celtic Cl YO26 49 A2
Cemetery Rd YO10 65 C1
Centurion Pk YO30 46 A3
Centurion Way YO30 46 A4
Chaldon Cl 4 YO32 11 C3
Chalfonts YO24 55 B2
Chaloner's Cres YO24 59 C4
Chaloner's Rd YO24 54 C1
Chancery Ct YO24 54 B4
Chancery Rise YO24 55 B4
Chantry Ave 14 YO26 16 B2
Chantry Cl YO24 54 B1
Chantry Gap 11 YO26 16 B2
Chantry Gr 13 YO26 16 B2
Chantry La YO23 61 A1
CHAPEL FIELDS 21 C3
Chapel Fields Rd YO26 21 C3
Chapel La YO23 26 B4
Chapel Row YO10 65 C1
Chapel Terr YO24 54 B4
Chapman Cl 1 YO32 6 B1
Chapmans Ct YO24 59 C3
Chapman's La YO30 9 A4
Chapter House St YO1 64 B3
Charles Moor YO31 52 B4
Charlton St YO23 56 B3
Chase Side Ct YO24 55 A1
Chatsworth Dr 16 YO32 11 B2
Chatsworth Terr 4 YO26 50 A1
Chaucer St 7 YO10 57 A4
Chaumont Way 1 YO32 17 C3
Chelkar Way YO30 45 B2
Chelwood Wlk 12 YO26 50 A1
Cherry Garth YO31 53 A2
Cherry Gr 16 YO26 16 B2
Cherry Hill La YO23 65 B1
Cherry La YO24 55 B1
Cherry Orch 7 YO32 11 A1
Cherry Paddock
22 Haxby YO32 11 A1
Kexby YO41 19 B3
Cherry St YO23 65 B1
Cherry Tree Ave
Newton-on-Ouse YO30 8 A3
York YO32 41 C1
Cherry Wood Cres YO19 62 A2
Cheshire Ave YO32 11 C3
Cheshire Cl 6 YO32 45 A3
Chesney Fields 4 YO24 54 C2
Chessingham Gdns YO24 60 A3
Chessingham Pk YO19 23 B3
Chestnut Ave YO31 52 B3
Chestnut Ct YO32 42 B2
Chestnut Gr YO26 49 B1
Chestnut Gr YO32 42 A1
Chestnuts The 15 YO32 11 A1
Cheviot Cl 1 YO32 47 B4
Chiltern Way YO32 42 B2
Chudleigh Rd 1 YO26 50 B2
Church Balk YO19 23 A4
Church Cl
Askham Bryan YO23 26 B4
5 Tollerton YO61 2 A4
Wheldrake YO19 37 C4
Church Farm Cl YO23 20 B3
Churchfield Dr 28 YO32 11 A2
Church Gn 3 YO41 31 B3
Church La
Appleton Roebuck YO23 33 B1
Bishopthorpe YO23 60 C1
Bolton Percy YO23 32 C1
Catton YO41 19 C1
Dunnington YO19 23 A4
4 Elvington YO41 31 B3
17 Haxby YO32 11 A2
Moor Monkton YO26 15 A3
Nether Poppleton YO26 44 A4
New Earswick YO32 42 B2
Poppleton YO26 16 C3
Skelton YO30 39 A2
10 Stamford Bridge YO41 19 C3
Strensall YO32 11 C4
Church La *continued*
Wheldrake YO19 37 C4
York YO1 65 B2
Church Mews 2 YO26 54 B4
Church Rd
Stamford Bridge YO41 19 C3
York YO10 53 C1
Church Rise YO19 18 B2
Church St
2 Copmanthorpe YO23 26 C2
Dunnington YO19 23 A4
York YO1 65 B2
Cinder La
Upper Poppleton YO26 16 C1
York YO26 50 C1
Cinder Mews YO26 50 C2
Claremont Terr YO31 64 B4
Clarence St YO31 64 B4
Clarendon Ct YO31 51 B4
Clarks Terr YO31 52 B3
CLAXTON 14 A4
Claygate YO31 53 A3
Clay Pl 3 YO24 54 C2
Clementhorpe YO23 65 B1
Clement St 4 YO23 65 B1
Cleveland St YO24 50 C1
Cleveland Terr YO32 42 B1
Cleveland Way YO32 47 B4
Clifford St YO1 65 B2
Clifford's Twr★ YO1 65 B1
CLIFTON 50 C4
Clifton YO30 64 A4
Clifton Dale YO30 50 C3
Clifton Gn YO30 50 C3
Clifton Gn Jun Sch YO30 51 A4
Clifton Gn Sch YO30 51 A4
Clifton Moorgate YO30 46 A4
Clifton Moor Gate YO30 45 C3
Clifton Moor Ind Pk★ YO30 40 C1
Clifton Moor Ret Pk YO30 45 A4
Clifton Moor Sh Ctr YO30 45 B4
CLIFTON PARK 50 B4
Clifton Pk Ave YO30 45 A1
Clifton Pl 3 YO30 50 C4
Clifton Prep Sch YO30 64 A4
Clifton Without Jun Sch YO30 45 B1
Clive Gr YO24 55 B3
Cloisters The YO31 64 C3
Cloisters Wlk YO31 64 C3
Close The YO30 45 B1
Cloverley Cl YO41 19 B3
Cobble Ct Mews YO24 65 A1
Cobham Way YO32 45 A4
COCK HILL 15 A3
Coeside YO24 59 A4
Coggan Cl YO23 56 A3
Coggan Way YO23 60 B1
Coledale Cl 2 YO30 45 B2
Colenso St YO23 65 B1
Cole St YO31 64 B4
College of Law YO23 61 A4
College Rd YO23 26 C3
College St YO1 64 B3
Colliergate YO1 65 B2
Collier Hag La YO23 25 A4
Collingwood Ave YO24 55 B3
Coll of Ripon & York St John YO31 52 A3
COLTON 33 A4
Colton La YO23 33 A3
Common Croft La YO26 16 A2
Common La
Dunnington YO19 23 B2
Sutton upon Derwent YO41 31 B1
Thorganby YO19 37 B2
Warthill YO19 18 B3
York YO10 58 A2
Common Rd YO19 23 B4
Comon Rd YO60 6 C2
Compton St YO30 50 C3
Concorde Pk YO30 45 C4
Coneycroft 10 YO19 23 B4
Coneygarth La YO19 23 A2
Coney St YO1 65 B2
Conifer Cl 6 YO32 46 C4
Coningham Ave 1 YO30 45 A3
Coniston Cl 1 YO30 45 A2
Coniston Dr YO10 53 A1
Connaught Way YO32 42 B3
Constantine Ave YO10 52 C1
Conway Cl 2 YO30 45 A4
Coombes Cl YO61 4 B4
Coopers Dr 14 YO23 26 C3
COPMANTHORPE 26 C2
Copmanthorpe La YO23 27 B3
Copmanthorpe Prim Sch YO23 26 C3
Copmanthorpe Sports Club YO23 26 C2
Copper beech Cl YO26 16 B1
Copper Beeches The 2 YO19 23 A4
Coppergate YO1 65 B2
Coppergate Sh Ctr YO1 65 B2
Coppergate Wlk YO1 65 B2
Coppice Cl 10 YO32 11 A2
Coppice The YO23 27 B3
Copwood Gr 20 YO32 11 A1
Corban La YO32 10 A3
Corban Way 21 YO32 10 C2
Corlett Ct YO24 54 B1
Cornaught Ct YO10 56 C1
Cornborough Av YO31 52 B3
Corner Cl 17 YO32 10 C2
Cornlands Rd YO24 54 A2
Cornwall Dr YO10 57 A1
Cornwood Way 30 YO32 11 A1
Cosmo Ave YO31 52 C2
Cotswold Way YO32 42 C2
Coulson Cl 5 YO32 6 B1
Count De Burgh Terr 4 YO23 56 A2
Courcey Gr YO26 49 B1
Courtneys YO19 30 C1
Courtyard The YO23 61 A1
Covert The YO24 60 B4
Cowper La YO23 27 B1
Coxlea Gr YO31 53 A3
Crabtree Gr 1 YO32 46 C4
Cranbrook Ave YO26 49 B2
Cranbrook Rd YO26 49 B2
Cranbrooks The YO19 30 B1
Cranfield Pl 4 YO24 54 B1
Crawley Way YO31 53 A3
Crescent The
Kexby YO41 24 B2
Stamford Bridge YO41 19 C3
York YO24 65 A1
Crichton Ave YO30 46 A1
Crinan Ct 3 YO32 42 B3
CROCKEY HILL 28 C2
Croft Ct YO23 60 C1
Croft Farm Cl 25 YO23 26 C3
Croftside 1 YO26 54 A4
Croftway 2 YO26 54 A4
Crombie Ave YO30 51 A4
Cromer St YO30 51 A4
Crompton Terr YO32 41 C3
Cromwell Rd YO1 65 B1
Crookland La YO32 11 B2
Crossfield Cres YO19 62 A3
Cross La Flaxton YO60 7 A1
Fulford YO19 62 B2
Crosslands Rd 2 YO10 57 A1
CROSS LANES 2 C4
Crossmoor La YO32 11 A3
Cross St 5 YO24 54 B4
Crossways YO10 58 B3
Crossway The 2 YO31 47 A1
Crummock 3 YO24 59 B4
Cumberland Cl 6 YO32 12 A3
Cumberland St YO1 65 B2
Cumbrian Ave 4 YO32 12 A3
Cundall Cl 6 YO32 6 B1
Curlew Glebe 8 YO19 23 A4
Curzon Terr YO23 56 A2
Custance Wlk YO23 65 A1
Cycle St 4 YO10 57 C4
Cygnet St YO23 65 A1
Cyprus Gr 37 YO32 11 A2

## D

Dalby Mead YO32 47 B2
Dale Dike Gr YO30 45 B3
Dale's La YO31 52 B3
Dale St YO23 65 A1
Dalguise Gr YO31 64 C4
Dalmally Cl YO24 59 A3
Dalton Hill YO19 30 C1

**Dalton Terr** YO24 .... 55 C4
**Dam Hill** YO23 ....... 20 A1
**Dam La** YO23 ........ 33 B1
**Damson Cl** YO26 ..... 50 A1
**Dane Ave** YO26 ...... 49 B2
**Danebury Cres** YO26 . 49 B1
**Danebury Ct** YO26 ... 49 B1
**Danebury Dr** YO26 ... 49 B1
**Danes Croft 2** YO10 . 56 C1
**Danesfort Ave** YO24 . 54 C3
**Danesgate** YO26 ..... 49 B1
**Danesmead** YO10 .... 56 C1
**Daneswell Cl 3**
YO41 .............. 19 C3
**Danum Dr** YO10 ...... 57 A1
**Danum Rd** YO10 ...... 57 A1
**Darbie Cl** YO32 ...... 41 C1
**Darfield Cl** YO32 ..... 6 A1
**Darley Cl 7** YO41 .... 19 C3
**Darling La** YO23 ..... 27 B1
**Darnborough St**
YO23 .............. 65 B1
**Darnbrook Wlk** YO31 53 A2
**Darwin Cl** YO41 ...... 47 A2
**Dauby La** YO41 ...... 31 A4
**Davygate** YO1 ....... 58 B2
**Daw La** YO23 ........ 33 C2
**Dawnay Garth** YO30 .. 9 A2
**Daysfoot Ct 9** YO10 . 57 A4
**Deacons Ct 6** YO23 . 26 C2
**Dealtry Ave 8** YO32 . 11 A1
**Deangate** YO1 ....... 64 B3
**Deanhead Gr 7**
YO30 .............. 45 A3
**Deans Cl** YO23 ...... 60 B1
**Dee Cl** YO24 ......... 59 A4
**Deepdale 5** YO24 .... 54 C1
**Deepfurrows La**
YO41 .............. 31 C4
**Deer Hill Gr** YO30 .... 45 B4
**Deerstone Way 22**
YO19 .............. 23 B4
**De Grey Ct** YO30 ..... 64 A4
**De Grey Pl 2** YO19 .. 27 C3
**De Grey St** YO31 .... 64 B4
**De Grey Terr**
York YO30 .......... 46 A4
York YO31 .......... 64 B4
**DEIGHTON** ........... 35 C4
**Delamere Cl 6** YO32 10 C2
**Dell The 13** YO10 ... 39 A2
**Del Pyke** YO31 ...... 64 C4
**Delwood** YO10 ....... 61 C4
**De Mowbray Ct** YO23 25 C4
**Dennison St** YO31 ... 64 C4
**Dennis St** YO1 ...... 65 C2
**Deramore Dr** YO10 .. 58 B4
**Deramore Dr W**
YO10 .............. 58 B4
**Derwent Ave** YO31... 52 B1
**Derwent Cl**
Elvington YO41 ...... 31 A4
**2** Stamford Bridge
YO41 .............. 19 C3
**Derwent Ct** YO41 .... 31 B3
**Derwent Dr** YO19 .... 27 B3
**Derwent Est** YO19 ... 23 A4
**Derwent Inf Sch**
YO10 .............. 53 A1
**Derwent Jun Sch**
YO10 .............. 53 A1
**Derwent Pk** YO10 .... 30 C1
**Derwent Rd** YO10 .... 56 C1
**Derwent Wlk** YO32 .. 42 B2
**Deveron Way** YO24 .. 59 A4
**Devon Pl** YO10 ...... 57 B4
**Dewsbury Ct** YO1 .... 65 A1
**Dewsbury Terr** YO1 .. 65 A1
**Diamond St** YO31 .... 64 C4
**Dickens Cl 1** YO32 .. 47 B2
**Dickson Rd 4** YO24 .. 54 A2
**Dijon Ave** YO24 ...... 54 B3
**Dikelands Cl 19** YO26 16 B2
**Dikelands La** YO26.... 16 B2
**Dike Ray Cl** YO32 .... 41 B4
**Dilys Gr 6** YO26 ..... 50 A1
**Disraeli Cl** YO32 ..... 47 A2
**Dixon La** YO1........ 65 C1
**Dixons Yd** YO1 ...... 65 C2
**Dodgson Terr** YO26.. 49 C1
**Dodsworth Ave** YO31 52 A4
**Doe Pk** YO30 ........ 45 A3
**Doherty Wlk** YO24 ... 54 B1
**Don Ave** YO24 ....... 59 A4
**Doriam Ave** YO31 .... 47 B3
**Doriam Dr** YO31 ..... 47 B3
**Dovecote Garth 5**
YO41 .............. 31 A3
**Dove St** YO23 ....... 65 A1
**Dower Chase** YO19 .. 35 C3
**Dower Pk** YO19 ...... 36 A3
**Drakes Cl** YO32 ..... 42 B2
**Drake St 2** YO23 .... 65 B1

**Drapers Croft**
**15** Copmanthorpe
YO23.............. 26 C3
Copmanthorpe YO23 .. 59 A1
**Driffield Terr** YO24 .. 55 C3
**Dringfield Cl 2**
YO24.............. 54 C1
**DRINGHOUSES** ...... 55 A1
**Dringhouses Prim Sch**
YO24.............. 55 B1
**Dringhouses Sports**
Club YO24 .......... 55 B1
**Dringthorpe Rd** YO24 60 B4
**Drome Rd** YO23 ..... 27 A2
**Drummond View**
YO23.............. 61 A1
**Dudley Mews** YO31 . 64 C4
**Dudley St** YO31 ..... 64 C4
**Dukes Wharf** YO23 .. 65 B1
**Duncombe Dr** YO32 .. 6 A1
**Duncombe La** YO32 .. 6 A1
**Duncombe Pl** YO1 ... 64 B3
**Dundas St** YO1 ...... 65 C2
**DUNNINGTON** ....... 23 B4
**Dunnington CE Prim**
Sch YO19 .......... 23 A4
**Durlston Dr** YO32 .... 11 C4
**Dykelands Cl** YO19 .. 37 B4
**Dykes La** YO23 ...... 26 C2

# E

**Earlit La** YO23 ...... 26 C1
**Earle St** YO31 ....... 64 C4
**Earlsborough Terr**
YO30.............. 64 A3
**EARSWICK** .......... 42 C4
**Earswick Chase**
YO32.............. 42 B4
**Earswick Village**
YO32.............. 42 B4
**Eason Rd** YO24 ...... 55 A1
**Eason View** YO24 .... 55 A1
**Eastbourne Gr** YO31 52 B2
**EAST COTTINGWITH**
.................. 38 B2
**Eastern Terr** YO31 .. 52 B2
**Eastfield Ave** YO32 .. 41 B4
**Eastfield Cres** YO10.. 58 B3
**Eastfield Ct** YO10 ... 58 B3
**Eastfield La** YO19.... 18 B1
**Eastholme Dr** YO30 . 64 A4
**Easthorpe Dr 6**
YO26.............. 16 C2
**Eastland Ave** YO10 .. 55 A3
**East Moor Gdns**
YO19.............. 62 B2
**East Mount Rd** YO24 65 A1
**East Parade** YO31 ... 52 B2
**Eastward Ave** YO10 . 62 A4
**East Way** YO31 ...... 47 A3
**Eaton Ct 8** YO24 .... 54 C3
**Ebor Ind Est** YO23 .. 64 C3
**Ebor Prep Sch** YO30 30 C2
**Ebor St** YO23 ....... 65 B1
**Ebor Way** YO26...... 16 C2
**Ebsay Dr** YO30 ...... 30 C1
**Eccles Cl** YO30 ...... 44 C3
**Eden Cl** YO24 ....... 59 B4
**Edgware Rd** YO10 ... 57 A3
**Edmund Wilson**
**Swimming Baths**
YO24.............. 54 C3
**Egremont Cl 11** YO41 19 C3
**Eighth Ave** YO31 .... 52 C3
**Elder Gr 38** YO32 ... 11 A2
**Eldon St** YO31 ...... 64 C4
**Eldon Terr** YO31 .... 64 C4
**Eldwick Cl** YO30 .... 45 B3
**Elgar Cl** YO31 ....... 47 A2
**Elliot Ct** YO10 ...... 61 C4
**Ellwood Ct** YO10 .... 56 B3
**Elma Gr 3** YO30 ..... 45 A3
**Elm End 8** YO32 .... 11 A2
**Elmfield Ave** YO31... 47 B3
**Elmfield Terr** YO31 .. 52 B4
**Elm Gr** YO31 ........ 47 B3
**Elmlands Gr** YO31 ... 47 B3
**Elmpark Vale** YO31 .. 47 C1
**Elmpark View** YO31 .. 47 C1
**Elmpark Way** YO31 .. 47 C1
**Elms The** YO32 ...... 17 C3
**Elm Tree Ave 9**
YO26.............. 16 B2
**Elmtree Gdns 3**
YO32.............. 42 A4
**Elston Cl** YO30 ...... 45 C1
**ELVINGTON** ......... 31 A4
**Elvington CE Prim Sch**
YO41.............. 31 A4
**Elvington Ind Est**
YO41.............. 30 C4
**Elvington La** YO19 ... 23 C2
**Elvington Pk** YO41.... 30 C4
**Elvington Terr** YO10 . 52 A1
**Elwick Gr** YO10 ..... 58 B3
**Embleton Dr 1** YO30 45 B2

**Emerald St** YO31 .... 64 C4
**Emily Mews** YO10 ... 52 A1
**Emmerson St 2**
YO31.............. 52 A2
**Enclosure Gdns 1**
YO10.............. 58 A2
**Endfields Rd 1** YO10 57 A1
**Enfield Cres 1** YO24 55 C4
**English Martyrs' RC**
Prim Sch YO24 ..... 55 B4
**Ennerdale Ave** YO31 . 53 A2
**ESCRICK** ............ 36 A2
**Escrick CE VC Prim Sch**
YO19.............. 35 C2
**Escrick Ct** YO19 ..... 36 A2
**Escrick Pk Gdns**
YO19.............. 36 A2
**Escrick St** YO10 ..... 65 C1
**Escrick Terr** YO10 ... 65 C1
**Eskdale Ave** YO10 ... 58 B2
**Esk Dr** YO26 ........ 44 A1
**Esplanade** YO26 ..... 65 A2
**Esplanade Ct** YO26 . 64 A3
**Etive Pl** YO24 ....... 59 A4
**Eton Dr 7** YO32 ..... 10 C2
**Etty Ave** YO10 ...... 52 C1
**Etty Cl 24** YO41 .... 19 C3
**Eva Ave** YO30 ....... 44 C3
**Evelyn Cres** YO30 ... 51 A4
**Exhibition Sq** YO1 ... 64 B3

# F

**Faber Cl 24** YO23 ... 26 C3
**Faber St** YO31 ...... 52 A2
**Fairfax 13** YO41 .... 19 C3
**Fairfax Cl** YO23 ..... 32 C1
**Fairfax Croft 8** YO23 26 C2
**Fairfax House★** YO1 65 C2
**Fairfax St** YO1 ...... 65 B1
**Fairfields Dr** YO30 .. 39 A2
**Fairway** YO30 ....... 45 C1
**Fairway Dr 18** YO26 . 16 B2
**Falcon Cl 12** YO32 .. 11 B2
**Falconer St 8** YO23 . 55 B4
**Falkland St** YO1 ..... 65 C1
**Falsgrave Cres** YO30 51 A4
**Farfield** YO26 ....... 49 B3
**Farfield La** YO19..... 18 A1
**Farfield Lane** YO19 .. 18 B1
**Farmers Way 28**
YO23.............. 26 C3
**Farmlands Rd 1**
YO24.............. 54 C1
**Farmstead Rise** YO32 41 C4
**Farndale Ave** YO10 .. 53 C1
**Farndale Cl 1** YO32 . 11 B2
**Farndale St** YO10 ... 56 C3
**Farrar St** YO10 ...... 56 C3
**Farriers Croft 18**
YO23.............. 26 C3
**Fawcett St** YO10 .... 65 C1
**Fawkes Dr** YO26 .... 49 B1
**Feasegate** YO1 ..... 65 B2
**Fellbrook Ave** YO26.. 49 A1
**Fenwick's La** YO10 .. 61 C4
**Fenwick St** YO23 .... 56 B3
**Ferguson Way** YO32 . 47 B2
**Fern Cl** YO32 ....... 42 C1
**Fern St** YO31 ....... 64 C4
**Fernway** YO10 ...... 58 B4
**Ferry Farm Cl 2**
YO19.............. 27 C1
**Ferry La**
Bishopthorpe YO23 .. 61 A1
Thorganby YO19 .... 38 A2
**Fetter La** YO1 ....... 65 B1
**Feversham Cres 4**
YO31.............. 51 B4
**Fewster Way** YO10 . 65 C1
**Fewston Dr 9** YO30 . 45 B2
**Field La** YO10 ....... 58 B3
**Field View** YO31 .... 56 B3
**Fifth Ave** YO31 ..... 52 B4
**Filey Terr** YO30 ..... 51 B4
**Finsbury Ave** YO23 .. 56 B2
**Finsbury St** YO23 ... 56 B2
**Firbank Cl** YO32 .... 11 C4
**Fir Heath Cl 5** YO24 . 54 B1
**First Ave** YO31 ..... 52 B3
**Firtree Cl**
**4** Earswick YO32 .. 42 B4
York YO26 .......... 52 A1
**Firwood Whin 5**
YO32.............. 47 B4
**Fishergate** YO10 .... 65 C1
**Fishergate Prim Sch**
YO10.............. 65 C1
**Flavian Gr** YO30 .... 45 B1
**Flaxman Ave** YO10 .. 52 B1
**Flaxman Croft** YO23 26 C3
**FLAXTON** ........... 7 B2
**Flaxton Pl** YO32 .... 12 A4
**Fleet Bank La** YO61 . 2 B2
**Fleming Ave 8** YO31 . 52 A1
**Fletcher Ct 14** YO32 11 A2

**Fletcher's Croft 6**
YO23.............. 27 A3
**Florence** YO30 ...... 44 C3
**Folks Cl 18** YO32 ... 11 B2
**Fordlands Cres** YO19 62 A2
**Fordlands Rd** YO19 .. 62 A2
**Forest Cl 27** YO32 .. 11 A2
**Foresters Wlk** YO41 . 19 B2
**Forester's Wlk** YO24 . 54 A2
**Forestgate** YO32 .... 41 B4
**Forest Gr** YO31...... 52 B3
**Forest La**
Fulford YO19 ....... 62 C3
Strensall YO32 ...... 5 C1
**Forest of Galtres Prim**
Sch YO30 ........... 9 B2
**Forest Way** YO31 ... 52 B3
**Forge Cl**
Huntington YO32 .... 47 C3
Wheldrake YO19 .... 37 C4
**Forge La** YO19 ..... 35 C4
**Forth St** YO26 ...... 50 B3
**Foss Bank** YO31 .... 64 C3
**Foss Ct** YO31........ 47 A2
**Foss Field La** YO23 .. 27 A1
**Fossgate** YO1 ....... 65 C2
**Foss Islands Rd** YO31 64 C3
**Fossland View 4**
YO32.............. 11 C4
**Fossway**
Stamford Bridge
YO41.............. 19 C2
York YO31 .......... 51 C4
**Foss Wlk** YO26 ..... 44 A1
**Foston CE VC Prim Sch**
YO6 ................ 7 C4
**Foston Gr 1** YO31 .. 47 B1
**Fountayne St** YO31 . 51 B4
**Fourth Ave** YO31 ... 52 A2
**Fox Covert** YO31 ... 47 B4
**Foxcroft 3** YO32 .... 41 B4
**Fox Garth** YO26 .... 16 C3
**Fox Glade** YO41 .... 19 B3
**Foxthorn Paddock**
YO10.............. 58 C4
**Foxton Cl** YO24 ..... 54 A1
**Foxwood La 3** YO24 . 54 B2
**Frances St** YO10 .... 56 C2
**Frazer Ct** YO30 ..... 45 A1
**Frederic St** YO30 ... 64 A3
**Friargate** YO1 ...... 65 B2
**Friargate Theatre**
YO1 ............... 65 B2
**Friars Cl** YO19 ...... 22 C4
**Friar's Wlk** YO31 ... 47 A1
**Front St** Naburn YO19 27 C2
York YO24 .......... 54 B4
**FULFORD** ........... 62 B4
**Fulford Cross** YO10 . 56 C2
**Fulfordgate** YO10 ... 62 A4
**Fulford Mews** YO10 . 62 A4
**Fulford Pk** YO10..... 61 C4
**Fulford Rd** YO10 .... 56 C1
**Fulford School** YO10 62 A4
**Furlong Rd 23** YO41 19 C3
**Furness Dr** YO30 ... 45 A2
**Furnwood 2** YO32 .. 41 C4
**Fylingdales Ave 6**
YO30.............. 45 A2

# G

**Gable Pk** YO23 ..... 20 B3
**Gainsborough Cl** YO23 6 A1
**Gale Farm Ct 6**
YO24.............. 54 B4
**Gale La**
Thorganby YO19 .... 37 B1
York YO24 .......... 54 B3
**Gale The** YO10 ..... 34 C1
**Galligap La** YO10 ... 59 B1
**Gallops The** YO41 ... 34 C2
**Galmanhoe La** YO30 64 A3
**Galtres Ave** YO31 ... 47 B3
**Galtres Gr** YO30 .... 50 B4
**Galtres Rd** YO31 .... 47 B3
**Ganton Pl** YO24 .... 59 A4
**Garbett Way 15** YO10 27 C3
**Garburn Gr 3** YO30 . 45 B1
**Garbutt Gr** YO26 .... 49 C2
**Gardeners Cl 26**
YO23.............. 26 C3
**Garden Flats La**
YO19.............. 23 A4
**Garden Pl** YO1 ...... 65 C2
**Garden St** YO31 .... 64 B4
**Garfield Terr** YO26 .. 50 B2
**Garland St 2** YO30 .. 51 B4
**Garlands The** YO10 . 45 C1
**Garnet Terr** YO26 ... 50 B2
**Garrowby View 5**
YO41.............. 19 C3
**Garrow Hill** YO10 ... 57 B3
**Garrow Hill Ave**
YO10.............. 57 A3
**Garth Cl** YO32 ...... 42 C1
**Garth End**
**20** Dunnington YO19 . 23 B4
YO32.............. 42 B1

**Garth Rd** YO32 ..... 42 B1
**Garths End** YO32 ... 11 B2
**Garth's End** YO10 ... 57 A1
**Garth Terr** YO30 .... 51 A4
**Garthway 4** YO32 ... 46 C4
**Gascoigne Wlk** YO23 65 B1
**Gatehead La** YO42... 38 C4
**GATE HELMSLEY** ... 19 A3
**Gateland Cl** YO32 ... 41 B4
**Gay Mdws** YO32 .... 17 C3
**Geldof Rd** YO32 ..... 47 B2
**Gennell La** YO60 .... 7 A2
**George Cayley Dr**
YO30.............. 45 C4
**George Ct** YO31 .... 64 C3
**George Hudson St**
YO1 ............... 65 B2
**George St** YO1 ...... 65 C2
**Gerard Ave** YO31 ... 52 C2
**Germany La** YO19 .. 62 A1
**Giles Ave** YO31 ..... 52 C2
**Gillamoor Ave** YO31 53 A2
**Gillygnwood Rd** YO30 45 B4
**Gipsey Cnr** YO19 ... 30 A4
**Girvan Cl** YO24 ..... 59 A4
**Givendale Gr 8**
YO10.............. 53 B1
**Glade The**
Escrick YO19 ....... 35 C3
York YO31 .......... 53 A4
**Gladstone St** YO31 . 64 C4
**Glaisby Ct** YO31 .... 52 C3
**Glaisdale** YO24 ..... 59 C4
**Glebe Ave** YO26 .... 49 C2
**Glebe Cl**
Bolton Percy YO23 .. 32 C1
**3** Strensall YO32 .. 12 A4
**Glebe Way 26** YO32 . 11 A2
**Glen Ave** YO31 ..... 52 A2
**Glen Cl** YO10 ....... 62 A3
**Glencoe St 1** YO30 . 51 A4
**Glen Rd** YO31 ...... 52 A2
**Glenridding** YO24 ... 59 C4
**Godwinsway 11** YO41 19 C3
**Goodramgate** YO1 .. 65 B2
**Goodwood Gr** YO24 . 55 B2
**Goose La** YO61 ...... 4 B2
**Goose Track La** YO60 4 B2
**Gordon St** YO10 .... 57 A4
**Gormire Ave 2** YO31 47 A3
**Gorse Hill** YO19 .... 23 B4
**Gorse Paddock** YO32 47 B3
**Gouthwaite Cl** YO30 45 B3
**Government House Rd**
YO30.............. 50 C3
**Gowans The** YO61 .. 4 B4
**Gower Rd** YO24 ..... 55 A1
**Grampian Cl 4** YO32 42 B2
**Granary Ct** YO1 ..... 65 C2
**Grange Cl** YO30 ..... 39 A2
**Grange Garth** YO10 . 56 C2
**Grange La** YO23..... 21 C2
**Grange St** YO10 .... 56 C3
**Grantham Dr** YO26 . 50 A1
**Grants Ave** YO10 ... 57 A1
**Granville Terr 4**
YO10.............. 57 A4
**Grape La** YO1 ....... 64 B3
**Grasmere Dr** YO10 . 53 A1
**Grasmere Gr 4** YO30 51 A4
**Grassholme** YO24 .. 59 B4
**Grayshon Dr** YO26 .. 49 A2
**Gray St** YO23 ....... 65 A1
**Great N Way** YO26 .. 44 A1
**Greenacres** YO32 ... 42 B1
**Green Cl** YO30...... 45 C1
**Greencliffe Dr** YO30 . 53 C3
**Greencroft Ct 14**
YO19.............. 23 B4
**Greencroft La 17**
YO19.............. 23 B4
**Green Dike 23** YO32 . 11 A1
**Green Dykes La** YO10 57 B4
**Greenfield Pk Dr**
YO31.............. 47 C2
**Greengales Ct** YO19 . 30 C1
**Greengales La** YO19 30 C1
**Green Hills** YO60.... 14 A4
**Green La** Acomb YO24 54 C3
Appleton Roebuck
YO23.............. 34 A3
Bishopthorpe YO23 .. 60 C3
Cottingwith YO42.... 38 B2
Rawcliffe YO30 ...... 45 C2
Wigginton YO32 .... 13 B4
**Greenlands Rd** YO19 23 B4
**Greensborough Ave 3**
YO30.............. 49 A2
**Greenshaw Dr** YO32 . 11 A1
**Greenside 13** YO19 . 23 B4
**Greenside Cl 25**
YO19.............. 23 B4
**Greenside Wlk 23**
YO19.............. 23 B4
**Green Sward** YO31 . 47 C1
**Green The**
**20** Dunnington YO19 . 23 B4

**Green The** *continued*
**1** Skelton YO30 ..... 39 A2
**2** Tollerton YO61 .... 2 A4
York YO26 .......... 54 B4
**Green Way** YO32 .... 42 B1
**Greenway The 2**
YO32.............. 41 B4
**Greenwood Gr** YO24 54 B1
**Gregory Cl** YO30 .... 39 B2
**Grenwich Cl 5** YO30 45 B4
**Gresley Ct 3** YO26 .. 49 A1
**Grey Cl** YO61 ........ 4 B4
**Greystoke Rd** YO32 . 41 B4
**Greystone Ct** YO32 .. 41 B4
**GRIMSTON** ......... 22 B3
**Grimston Bar** YO19 . 22 B3
**Grimwith Garth** YO30 45 B3
**Grosvenor House**
YO30.............. 64 A4
**Grosvenor Pk** YO30 . 64 A4
**Grosvenor Rd** YO30 . 64 A4
**Grosvenor Terr** YO30 64 A4
**Grove Gdns 22** YO26 . 16 B2
**Groves Ct** YO31 ..... 64 C3
**Groves La** YO31 ..... 64 C3
**Grove Terr La** YO31 . 64 C4
**Grove The** YO24 .... 60 A3
**Grove View** YO30 ... 50 C3

# H

**Haddon Cl** YO24 .... 54 B3
**Hadrian Ave** YO10 .. 58 A4
**Hagg La** Colton LS24 . 26 A1
Dunnington YO19 ... 23 B1
**Haley's Terr** YO31.... 46 C1
**Halifax Ct 7** YO30 .. 45 C2
**Halifax Way** YO41 ... 30 C4
**Halladale Cl 1** YO24 . 59 A4
**Hallard Way 7** YO32 12 A4
**Hallcroft La 17** YO23 . 26 C3
**Halfield Rd** YO31 .... 52 A2
**HALL GARTH** ....... 23 B3
**Hall Pk** YO10 ....... 58 A2
**Hall Rise 12** YO32 ... 11 B2
**Hambleton Ave** YO10 53 B1
**Hambleton Terr**
YO31.............. 51 B4
**Hambleton View**
**10** Haxby YO32 ..... 10 C2
**4** Tollerton YO61 .... 2 A4
**Hambleton Way**
YO32.............. 47 B4
**Hamilton Dr** YO24 .. 55 B3
**Hamilton Dr E** YO24 . 55 B3
**Hamilton Dr W** YO24 54 C3
**Hamilton Dr W** YO24 55 A3
**Hammerton Cl 3**
YO26.............. 16 B1
**Hampden St** YO1 ... 65 B1
**Hampson Gdns** YO30 46 A1
**Hampton Gdns** YO30 46 B1
**Handley Cl** YO30 .... 45 C3
**Hanover St E 5**
YO26.............. 50 B2
**Hanover St W 7**
YO26.............. 50 B2
**Hansom Pl** YO31 .... 51 B4
**Harcourt Cl**
**1** Bishopthorpe
YO23.............. 27 C3
Wheldrake YO19..... 37 B4
**Harcourt St 1** YO31 . 52 A2
**Harden Cl** YO30 ..... 45 B4
**Hardisty Mews** YO26 50 C1
**Hardrada Way 8**
YO41.............. 19 C2
**Harewood Cl**
Rawcliffe YO30 ...... 44 C3
**5** Wigginton YO32 . 13 B4
**Harewood Way** YO10 52 B1
**Harington Ave** YO10 52 B1
**Harland Cl** YO61..... 4 B4
**Harlow Cl** YO24 ..... 54 B3
**Harlow Rd** YO24 ... 55 A4
**Harold Ct** YO24 ..... 54 C4
**Harolds Way 1** YO41 19 C2
**Harrison St** YO31.... 52 B3
**Harrow Glade 5**
YO30.............. 45 C2
**Hartoft St** YO10 .... 56 C3
**Hassacarr La** YO19 . 23 B3
**Hastings Cl 4** YO30 . 45 C2
**Hatfield Cl 4** YO30 .. 45 A4
**Hatfield Wlk** YO24 .. 54 A1
**Hatters Cl 21** YO23 . 26 C3
**Haughton Rd** YO30 . 51 B4
**Hauling La** YO23 .... 27 B1
**Haverah Ct** YO30 ... 45 B3
**Hawkshead Cl 3**
YO24.............. 54 A1
**Hawthorne Ave 12**
YO31.............. 11 A2
**Hawthorne Gr** YO31 . 52 A2
**Hawthorne Mews**
YO32.............. 5 C1

Hawthorn Gr YO31 . . 52 A2
Hawthorn Pl YO32 . . 42 A1
Hawthorn Spinney
YO32 . . . . . . . . . . . . 47 A4
Hawthorn St 1 YO31 52 A2
Hawthorn Terr YO32 . 41 C1
Hawthorn Terr Cent 2
YO32 . . . . . . . . . . . 46 C4
Hawthorn Terr N
YO32 . . . . . . . . . . . 46 C4
Hawthorn Terr S
YO32 . . . . . . . . . . . 41 C1
HAXBY . . . . . . . . . . 11 A1
Haxby Moor Rd
Haxby YO32 . . . . . 11 B4
Towthorpe YO32 . . . 11 C4
Haxby Rd Clifton YO31 46 C2
New Earswick YO32 . 41 C3
York YO31 . . . . . . . . 64 B4
Haxby Rd Prim Sch
YO31 . . . . . . . . . . . 51 C4
Hayforth Cl YO30 . . . 45 C3
Hazel Cl YO32 . . . . . 46 C3
Hazel Ct YO31 . . . . . 52 A1
Hazel Garth YO31 . . . 53 A4
Hazelmere Ct YO32 . . 47 A4
Hazelnut Gr YO32 . . . 46 A3
Hazelwood Ave YO10 53 C1
Headland Cl 1 YO32 11 A2
Headlands Prim Sch
YO32 . . . . . . . . . . . 11 A1
Headley Cl 2 YO30 . . 46 A2
Healey Gr YO31 . . . . 47 B1
Heath Cl 2 YO24 . . . 55 B3
Heath Croft YO10 . . . 62 B4
Heather Bank
13 Stamford Bridge
YO41 . . . . . . . . . . . 19 C3
York YO10 . . . . . . . 53 B1
Heather Cl YO32 . . . 42 C1
Heather Croft 4
YO31 . . . . . . . . . . . 47 A3
Heathfield Rd 1
YO10 . . . . . . . . . . . 57 C4
Heath Moor Dr YO10 57 B1
Heath Ride YO32 . . . . 6 A1
Hebdon Rise 2
YO26 . . . . . . . . . . . 49 C1
Height Lands La
YO23 . . . . . . . . . . . 20 C3
Helmsdale YO24 . . . . 59 B3
Helmsley Gr 1 YO32 10 C2
Hemlock Ave YO32 . . 47 A2
Hempland Ave YO31 . 52 C3
Hempland Dr YO31 . . 52 C4
Hempland Jun Sch
YO31 . . . . . . . . . . . 53 A3
Hempland La YO31 . . 52 C4
Hempland Prim Sch
YO31 . . . . . . . . . . . 52 C3
Hendon Garth YO30 . 45 C2
Herbert St 13 YO10 . . 57 A4
Herberts Way YO31 . . 52 B4
Herdsman Dr 5
YO23 . . . . . . . . . . . 27 A3
Herdsman Rd 3
YO24 . . . . . . . . . . . 54 C1
Herdwick Cl 1 YO30 46 A2
Herman Wlk YO24 . . 54 B1
Heron Ave YO24 . . . . 54 B1
Heron Rise YO32 . . . 42 B2
Hesketh Bank YO10 . 58 C4
Heslin Cl 13 YO32 . . 11 A1
HESLINGTON . . . . . 58 A2
Heslington Croft
YO10 . . . . . . . . . . . 62 B4
Heslington Ct 2
YO10 . . . . . . . . . . . 58 A2
Heslington La
Heslington YO10 . . . 57 C2
York YO10 . . . . . . . 57 B4
Heslington Rd YO10 . 57 A4
HESSAY . . . . . . . . . 15 B1
Hessay Pl 2 YO26 . . 21 C3
Hetherton St YO30 . . 64 A3
Hewley Ave YO10 . . . 52 C1
HEWORTH . . . . . . . 52 C3
Heworth YO31 . . . . . 52 C3
Heworth CE Prim Sch
YO31 . . . . . . . . . . . 52 B3
Heworth Gn YO31 . . . 64 C4
Heworth Hall Dr
YO31 . . . . . . . . . . . 52 B3
Heworth Mews YO31 52 A3
Heworth Pl YO31 . . . 52 B3
Heworth Rd YO31 . . . 52 B3
Heworth Village
YO31 . . . . . . . . . . . 52 C3
HIGH CATTON . . . . . 19 A4
High Catton Rd YO41 19 C1
Highcliffe Ct YO30 . . 50 C3
High Field YO10 . . . . 53 C1
Highgrove Cl 7
YO30 . . . . . . . . . . . 45 A4
High Garth YO41 . . . 31 C4
Highlands Ave 13
YO32 . . . . . . . . . . . 12 A4
Highmoor Cl YO24 . . 54 C1

High Moor La YO30 . . . .2 B1
Highmoor Rd YO24 . . 54 C1
High Newbiggin St
YO31 . . . . . . . . . . . 58 A4
High Oaks YO31 . . . . 53 A4
High Ousegate YO1 . . 64 B3
High Petergate YO1 . 64 B3
Highthorn Rd YO31 . . 47 A3
Hilbeck Gr YO31 . . . . 53 A3
Hilbra Ave YO32 . . . . 41 C3
Hilda St 3 YO10 . . . . 57 A4
Hillary Garth 6
YO23 . . . . . . . . . . . 27 A3
Hill Crest YO19 . . . . . 18 B2
Hillcrest Ave YO26 . . 16 C2
Hill Crest Gdns YO24 55 B2
Hillgarth Ct YO41 . . 31 A3
Hillsborough Terr 5
YO30 . . . . . . . . . . . 51 B4
Hillside Cl YO41 . . . . 46 A3
Hill St YO24 . . . . . . . 55 A4
Hill View YO31 . . . . . 53 A4
Hinton Ave 1 YO24 . 54 B1
Hobgate YO24 . . . . . 54 C4
Hob Moor Com Prim
Sch YO24 . . . . . . . 54 C3
Hob Moor Dr YO24 . . 55 A3
Hob Moor Jun Sch
YO24 . . . . . . . . . . . 55 A3
Hob Moor Oaks Sch
YO26 . . . . . . . . . . . 49 B3
Hobmoor Terr YO24 . 55 A3
Hobson Cl 15 YO23 . 27 A3
Hodgson La YO26 . . . 16 B1
Holburns Croft 3
YO26 . . . . . . . . . . . 49 B3
HOLGATE . . . . . . . . 55 A4
Holgate Bridge Gdn 7
YO24 . . . . . . . . . . . 55 C4
Holgate Lodge Dr
YO26 . . . . . . . . . . . 50 A1
Holgate Rd YO24 . . . 54 C4
Hollis Cres YO32 . . . 12 A3
Holly Bank Gr 3
YO24 . . . . . . . . . . . 55 A3
Holly Bank Rd YO24 . 55 B3
Holly Cl YO25 . . . . . . 27 B1
Hollyrood Rd YO30 . . 45 A4
Holly Terr YO10 . . . . 56 C2
Holly Tree Croft 2
YO19 . . . . . . . . . . . 38 A4
Holly Tree Garth
YO19 . . . . . . . . . . . 18 A4
Holly Tree La
Dunnington YO19 . . 23 B4
13 Haxby YO32 . . . 11 B4
Holmefield La YO10 . 57 C2
HOLME GREEN . . . . 31 B4
Holme Green Rd
YO23 . . . . . . . . . . . 33 B1
Holroyd Ave YO31 . . 53 A2
Holtby La YO19 . . . . . 54 A1
HOLTBY . . . . . . . . . 18 B2
Holtby La Holtby YO19 17 C2
Stockton-on-the-Forest
YO32 . . . . . . . . . . . 17 C2
Homefield Cl 2
YO23 . . . . . . . . . . . 27 A3
Homestead Ct 2
YO32 . . . . . . . . . . . 47 B2
Hope St YO10 . . . . . . 65 C4
HOPGROVE . . . . . . . 48 C3
Hopgrove La N YO32 . 48 B2
Hopgrove La S YO32 . 17 B2
Hornbeam Cl YO30 . . 46 A3
Horner St YO30 . . . . 51 A4
Hornsey Garth 25
YO32 . . . . . . . . . . . 11 A2
Horseman Ave 11
YO23 . . . . . . . . . . . 26 C3
Horseman Cl 8
YO23 . . . . . . . . . . . 26 C3
Horseman Dr 8
YO23 . . . . . . . . . . . 26 C3
Horseman La YO23 . . 26 C3
Horseshoe The YO26 . 60 A4
Horsfield Way YO19 . 23 B4
Horsman Ave YO10 . . 65 C1
Hospital Fields Rd
YO10 . . . . . . . . . . . 56 C2
Hospitium The * YO1 64 A3
Hotham Ave YO24 . . 54 A3
Hothams Ct YO1 . . . 65 C2
Houndsway 6 YO24 . 59 B4
Howard Dr YO31 . . . 48 A2
Howard Link YO30 . . 44 C3
Howard Rd YO32 . . . 12 A1
Howard St YO10 . . . 56 C3
Howden La YO19 . . . 28 B2
Howe Hill Cl YO26 . . 50 A1
Howe Hill Rd YO24 . . 54 C4
Hubert St 2 YO23 . . 56 A2
Huby Rd YO61 . . . . . . 4 A4
Huby Ct YO41 . . . . . 19 C3
Hudson Cres 2
YO30 . . . . . . . . . . . 50 C4
Hudson St 6 YO30 . . 51 B4

Hull Rd
Osbaldwick YO10 . . 58 C4
York YO10 . . . . . . . 58 A4
Humber Dr 5 YO32 . 12 A3
Hungate YO1 . . . . . . 65 C2
Hunt Ct YO31 . . . . . 64 C3
Hunters Cl
Dunnington YO19 . . 23 A4
27 Haxby YO32 . . . 11 A1
Hunters Way YO24 . 41 A1
Hunters Wood Way 2
YO19 . . . . . . . . . . . 23 B4
HUNTINGTON . . . . . 47 A4
Huntington Mews
YO31 . . . . . . . . . . . 51 C4
Huntington Prim Sch
YO32 . . . . . . . . . . . 42 B1
Huntington Rd YO31 . 64 C4
Huntington Sec Sch
YO32 . . . . . . . . . . . 47 A4
Huntington Sports Club
YO32 . . . . . . . . . . . 42 C2
Huntsman's La YO41 . 19 B3
Huntsman's Wlk
YO24 . . . . . . . . . . . 54 A2
Hurns La YO30 . . . . . . 9 C1
Hurricane Way YO30 . 45 A4
Hurst's Yd YO1 . . . . 65 C2
Hutton Cl 3 YO26 . . 16 C2
Hyrst Gr YO31 . . . . . 52 A3

**I**

Ikin Way YO32 . . . . 42 B1
Ilton Garth YO30 . . . 45 C3
Ingleborough Ave
YO10 . . . . . . . . . . . 53 A1
Ingleton Wlk 3
YO31 . . . . . . . . . . . 52 C2
Ingrish La YO23 . . . 25 B2
Ings La
Cottingwith YO42 . . 38 B2
Lillings Ambo YO60 . . 6 B3
Nether Poppleton
YO26 . . . . . . . . . . . 44 A2
Thorganby YO19 . . . 38 A2
Tollerton YO61 . . . . . 2 A3
Wheldrake YO19 . . . 38 A4
York YO10 . . . . . . . 57 C2
Ings Rd YO19 . . . . . 38 A1
Ings View YO30 . . . . 44 C3
Inman Terr YO26 . . . 54 A4
Innovation Cl YO10 . 58 A1
Innovation Way YO10 58 A3
Intake Ave YO31 . . . 46 B1
Intake La
Acaster Malbis YO23 . 34 B4
Dunnington YO19 . . 23 B4
Invicta Ct YO24 . . . 54 A1
Irvine Way YO24 . . . 59 A4
Irwin Ave YO31 . . . . 52 A3
Iver Cl YO30 . . . . . . 49 B2
Ivy Pl YO32 . . . . . . . 46 C4

**J**

Jackson St YO31 . . . 64 C4
Jackson's Wlk YO23 . 28 C4
Jacobi Cl YO30 . . . . 51 A4
James Backhouse Pl
YO24 . . . . . . . . . . . 55 A4
James Nicholson Way
YO30 . . . . . . . . . . . 45 C4
James Nicolson Link
YO30 . . . . . . . . . . . 45 C4
James St YO10 . . . . 52 A1
Jamieson Terr YO23 . 56 A2
Jasmine Cl YO32 . . . 46 C4
Jaywick Cl YO32 . . . . 6 A1
Jedwell Cl YO32 . . . 41 C2
Jennifer Gr 4 YO23 . 55 B3
Jervis Rd YO24 . . . . 54 B3
Jervis Rd YO41 . . . . 31 B2
Jewbury YO31 . . . . . 64 C3
Jockey La YO32 . . . . 47 B3
John St YO31 . . . . . . 64 B3
JORVIK * YO1 . . . . . 65 C2
Jorvik Cl YO30 . . . . 49 B2
Joseph Rowntree Sec
Sch YO32 . . . . . . . 42 A2
Jubbergate YO1 . . . . 65 C2
Jubilee Court 6 YO61 2 A4
Jubilee St 33 YO23 . 11 A1
Jubilee Terr YO26 . . 56 A4
Julia Ave YO32 . . . . 47 B3
Juniper Cl YO32 . . . 46 C4
Jute Rd YO26 . . . . . 49 A2

**K**

Kathryn Ave YO32 . . 47 C3
Keats Cl YO30 . . . . . 45 B1
Keble Dr 12 YO23 . . 27 C3
Keble Gdns YO23 . . . 27 C2

Keble Pk Cres 13
YO23 . . . . . . . . . . . 27 C3
Keble Pk N YO23 . . . 27 C2
Keble Pk S YO23 . . . 27 C2
Keepers Way 11
YO23 . . . . . . . . . . . 55 B1
Keith Ave YO32 . . . . 42 C1
Keldale 4 YO32 . . . . 11 B2
Kempton Cl 2 YO24 . 54 C2
Kendal Cl YO19 . . . . 23 B4
Kendrew Cl 3 YO32 . 47 B4
Kenlay Cl YO31 . . . . 41 C1
Kennedy Cl 4 YO32 . 11 B2
Kenrick Pl 11 YO26 . 49 A2
Kensal Rise YO10 . . 56 C3
Kensington Cl 1
YO24 . . . . . . . . . . . 55 B1
Kensington Rd YO30 . 44 C3
Kensington St YO30 . 56 A4
Kentmere Dr YO30 . . 56 A2
Kensington Way 7
YO26 . . . . . . . . . . . 49 A1
Kerris Cl YO32 . . . . . 46 C3
Kerver La YO19 . . . . 23 B4
Kestrel Wood Way
YO31 . . . . . . . . . . . 47 B3
Keswick Way 8
YO32 . . . . . . . . . . . 42 B2
Kettlestring La YO30 . 45 C4
KEXBY . . . . . . . . . . 20 C1
Kexby Ave YO10 . . . 57 B4
Kexby Bridge* YO41 23 C2
Key Way YO19 . . . . . 62 B2
Kilburn Rd YO10 . . . 56 C3
Kimberlows Wood Hill
YO10 . . . . . . . . . . . 58 B4
Kinbrace Dr YO30 . . 45 A3
Kings Acre YO31 . . . 53 B2
Kingsclere YO32 . . . 42 B3
Kings Ct YO1 . . . . . . 65 B2
Kingsland Terr 11
YO26 . . . . . . . . . . . 56 A4
Kings Moor Rd YO32 17 C3
King's Sq YO1 . . . . . 65 C2
King's Staith YO1 . . 65 B2
King St YO1 . . . . . . . 65 B2
Kingsthorpe YO24 . . 54 B1
Kingsway N YO30 . . 51 C4
Kingsway W YO24 . . 54 B2
Kingswood Gr YO24 . 54 B4
Kir Cres YO24 . . . . . 54 B4
Kirk Balk La YO60 . . 14 A4
Kirkcroft 11 YO32 . . 11 A1
Kirkdale Rd YO10 . . 58 A4
Kirkham Ave 1
YO31 . . . . . . . . . . . 47 A1
Kirklands YO32 . . . . 42 A2
Kirkstone Dr YO31 . . 52 C3
Kirk View YO24 . . . . 54 B4
Kirkwell YO23 . . . . . 60 C1
Kitchener St YO31 . . 51 C4
Kitty Garth YO19 . . . 37 C4
KNAPTON . . . . . . . . 21 C4
Knapton Cl 1 YO32 . 12 A3
Knapton La YO26 . . . 49 A1
KNAVESMIRE . . . . . 60 C4
Knavesmire Cres
YO23 . . . . . . . . . . . 56 A2
Knavesmire Prim Sch
YO23 . . . . . . . . . . . 55 C2
Knavesmire Rd YO23 55 C2
Knoll The YO24 . . . . 54 A4
Kyle Cl 3 YO61 . . . . . 2 A4
Kyle Way YO30 . . . . 45 B1
Kyme St YO1 . . . . . . 65 B1

**L**

Laburnum Cl YO23 . 20 B3
Laburnum Garth 6
YO31 . . . . . . . . . . . 52 A3
Laburnum Way YO19 34 C1
Lady Anne Ct YO30 . 44 C1
Lady Hamilton Gdns
YO30 . . . . . . . . . . . 55 A3
Lady Mill Garth YO30 46 A1
Lady Peckitts Yd YO1 65 B2
Lady Rd YO30 . . . . . 51 A4
Ladysmith Mews 13
YO31 . . . . . . . . . . . 11 C4
Lady Wortley Pl
YO23 . . . . . . . . . . . 61 A3
Lakeside YO10 . . . . 34 B4
Lakeside Gr 1 YO32 . 6 A1
Lambert Ct YO1 . . . 65 B1
Lamel St YO10 . . . . 57 A3
Lamplugh Cr 9
YO19 . . . . . . . . . . . 27 C3
Lancar Cl YO32 . . . . 10 C2
Lancaster Way YO32 . 11 C3
Landalewood Rd
YO30 . . . . . . . . . . . 45 B3
Landau Cl YO30 . . . 45 B1

Landing La
22 Haxby YO32 . . . 11 B2
Haxby YO32 . . . . . 42 A4
York YO26 . . . . . . . 50 A3
Landings The 21
YO32 . . . . . . . . . . . 11 B2
Lane The YO41 . . . . 19 A3
Lang Ave YO10 . . . . 52 C1
Langdale Ave YO31 . 53 A3
Langholme Dr YO26 . 49 B3
Langley Ct 2 YO32 . 42 B3
Lang Rd
Bishopthorpe YO23 . 60 B1
York YO26 . . . . . . . 50 A3
Langrickgate La
YO42 . . . . . . . . . . . 38 B2
Langsett Gr YO30 . . 45 B4
Langton Ct 1 YO41 . 11 C3
Lansdowne Terr 5
YO10 . . . . . . . . . . . 57 A4
Lansdown Way 7
YO30 . . . . . . . . . . . 45 A3
Larchfield YO31 . . . . 53 B4
Larch Way 35 YO32 . 11 A1
Larkfield Cl 5 YO23 . 24 C3
Lasenby Cl YO32 . . . 41 C2
Lastingham Terr
YO10 . . . . . . . . . . . 56 C3
Lavender Gr YO26 . . 50 A2
Laverocks Ind Est
YO41 . . . . . . . . . . . 31 A4
Lawnswood Dr YO30 45 B1
Lawnway YO31 . . . . 52 C4
Lawrence St YO10 . . 57 A4
Lawson Rd YO24 . . . 60 B4
LAYERTHORPE . . . . 52 A1
Layerthorpe YO31 . . 52 A1
Leadley Croft 17
YO23 . . . . . . . . . . . 26 C2
Lead Mill La YO1 . . 65 C1
Leake St YO10 . . . . 57 A4
Learmans Way 9
YO23 . . . . . . . . . . . 27 A3
Lea Way YO32 . . . . 42 C1
Leeman Rd YO26 . . 56 B4
Leeside YO24 . . . . . 54 A2
Leicester Way YO1 . 65 C1
Leighton Croft 3
YO30 . . . . . . . . . . . 45 B2
Leisure Pk YO32 . . . 47 B3
Lendal YO1 . . . . . . . 65 B2
Lerecroft Rd YO24 . 54 C1
Lesley Ave YO10 . . . 57 A1
Leven Rd YO24 . . . . 54 A1
Levisham St YO10 . . 56 C3
Leyes The YO10 . . . 53 B1
Leyfield Cl 1 YO32 . 11 C2
Leyland Rd YO31 . . 52 C4
Library Sq YO1 . . . . 64 B3
Lichfield Ct 6 YO23 . 56 A1
Lidgett Cl YO23 . . . 27 C1
Lidgett Gr Sch YO26 49 A3
Lilac Ave
Appleton Roebuck
YO23 . . . . . . . . . . . 33 B2
York YO10 . . . . . . . 57 B1
Lilac Gr YO32 . . . . . 41 C1
Lilbourne Dr YO30 . . 45 C2
Lilling Ave 3 YO31 . 54 B1
Lilling Gr YO60 . . . . 7 A4
Lilling Low La YO32 . 8 C2
Limegarth 10 YO26 . 43 B1
Limes Ct YO31 . . . . 52 A4
Lime Tree Ave YO32 . 41 C1
Lime Tree Mews 19
YO19 . . . . . . . . . . . 23 B4
Lincoln St YO26 . . . 56 A4
Lindale 1 YO24 . . . 59 B4
Linden Cl YO32 . . . . 42 B2
Linden Gr 1 YO30 . . 45 C1
Lindley St YO30 . . . 55 A4
Lindley Wood Gr
YO30 . . . . . . . . . . . 45 B3
Lindsey Ave YO26 . . 56 A3
Lingcroft La YO19 . . 28 B1
Lingfield Cres YO10 . 58 B3
Link Ave YO30 . . . . 55 B1
Link Rd YO10 . . . . . 57 A3
Link Rd Ct YO19 . . . 53 C1
Link The
1 Copmanthorpe
YO23 . . . . . . . . . . . 26 C2
York YO10 . . . . . . . 58 B3
Linley Ave YO24 . . . 54 B4
Linnet Way YO24 . . 54 A1
Linton on Ouse Prim
Sch YO30 . . . . . . . 2 A2
Linton Rd 8 YO26 . . 16 C2
Linton St 9 YO26 . . 56 A4
Linton Woods YO30 . . 9 C4
Lister Way YO30 . . . 50 C4
Litchfield Ct YO24 . . 55 C1
Littlefield Cl 5 YO19 23 B4
Little Garth 8 YO26 . 16 C2

Little Hallfield Rd
YO31 . . . . . . . . . . . 52 A2
Little La 11 YO32 . . 11 A2
Little Meadows 31
YO31 . . . . . . . . . . . 53 A4
Little Stonegate YO1 64 B3
Littlethorpe Cl 7
YO32 . . . . . . . . . . . 6 A1
Livingstone St YO26 . 50 B2
Lloyd Cl YO10 . . . . . 58 A2
Lochrin Cl YO41 . . . 19 C3
Lochrin Pl 16 YO26 . 49 A1
Lockey Croft 1
YO32 . . . . . . . . . . . 11 A1
Lockwood St YO31 . . 64 C3
Lockyer Cl 4 YO30 . . 45 C1
Lofthouse La YO41 . . 24 C4
Long Cl La YO10 . . . 65 C1
Longcroft 2 YO32 . . 11 A2
Longfield Terr YO30 . 64 A3
Long Furrow 28
YO32 . . . . . . . . . . . 11 A1
Long Lane YO26 . . . 24 C3
Long Ridge Dr 10
YO26 . . . . . . . . . . . 16 C2
Long Ridge La YO26 . 16 C2
Longwood Link 8
YO30 . . . . . . . . . . . 45 A4
Longwood Rd YO30 . 45 B4
Lord Deramore's Prim
Sch YO10 . . . . . . . 58 B2
Lord Mayor's Wlk
YO31 . . . . . . . . . . . 64 B4
Lords La YO26 . . . . 16 A3
Lords Moor La YO32 . 12 B4
Loriners Dr 27 YO23 . 26 C3
Lorne St YO23 . . . . 56 A2
Lorraine Ave 3
YO41 . . . . . . . . . . . 31 A3
Love La
Nunthorpe YO10 . . . 56 B1
York YO24 . . . . . . . 55 C1
LOW CATTON . . . . . 19 B1
Low Croft 6 YO32 . . 11 C4
Lower Darnborough St
YO23 . . . . . . . . . . . 65 B1
Lower Friargate YO1 65 B2
Lower Priory St YO1 65 A1
Loweswater Rd 6
YO30 . . . . . . . . . . . 45 C1
Low Farm Cl YO23 . 32 C1
Lowfield Dr YO32 . . 11 C2
Lowfield La YO23 . . 21 C3
Low Fields Dr YO24 . 54 B4
Lowfield Sec Sch
YO24 . . . . . . . . . . . 54 B4
Low Gn YO26 . . . . . 26 C2
Lowick YO24 . . . . . . 59 B4
Low Mill Cl YO10 . . 58 C2
Low Moor Ave 3
YO10 . . . . . . . . . . . 57 B1
Low Moor La
Askham Richard
YO23 . . . . . . . . . . . 25 C4
Hessay YO26 . . . . . 15 B1
Low Poppleton La
YO26 . . . . . . . . . . . 49 A4
Lowther St YO31 . . 64 C4
Lowther Terr YO1 . . 56 A4
Low Well YO19 . . . . 37 B4
Low Westfield Rd
YO23 . . . . . . . . . . . 54 A4
Loxley Cl YO10 . . . . 45 B3
Lucas Ave YO30 . . . 45 B3
Lucombe Way YO32 . 41 C1
Lumley Rd YO30 . . . 45 A4
Lund Cl 24 YO32 . . 11 A1
Lundgreen La YO61 . . 3 C4
Lundy Cl 10 YO30 . . 45 C2
Lycett Rd YO24 . . . 60 B3
Lydham Cl 8 YO24 . 54 B1
Lyndale Ave YO10 . . 58 B3
Lyndon Way YO24 . . 54 B1
Lynwood Ave 9
YO23 . . . . . . . . . . . 26 C3
Lynwood Cl YO23 . . 11 C4
Lynwood View 6
YO23 . . . . . . . . . . . 26 C3
Lysander Cl YO30 . . 45 C4

**M**

Mcan Cl YO10 . . . . 53 C1
McArthur Designer
Outlet YO19 . . . . . 61 C1
MacLagan Rd YO23 . 60 B1
Magnolia Gr YO32 . . 46 C3
Maida Gr YO10 . . . . 56 C3

Main Ave YO31 ...... 52 B2
Main St
Appleton Roebuck
  YO23 ............... 33 B2
Askham Bryan YO23 .. 26 B4
Bilbrough YO23 ....... 25 B2
Bishopthorpe YO23 ... 60 C1
Copmanthorpe YO23 .. 26 C2
Cottingwith YO42 .... 38 B2
Deighton YO19 ....... 35 C4
Elvington YO41 ....... 31 B3
Escrick YO19 ......... 36 A2
Heslington YO10 ...... 58 A2
Hessay YO26 ......... 15 A1
Knapton YO26 ........ 21 C4
**1** Naburn YO19 ...... 27 C1
Nunthorpe YO10 ...... 56 C1
Poppleton YO26 ...... 16 B2
Shipton YO30 .......... 9 B2
  Stamford Bridge YO41 . 19 C3
Wheldrake YO19 ...... 37 B4
Malbys Gr **4** YO23 .. 26 C2
Malham Gr YO31 ..... 53 A2
Mallard Way **11** YO32 11 B2
Mallory Cl YO32 ..... 41 C1
Malt Kiln La YO23 ... 33 B2
Malton Ave YO31 .... 52 A3
Malton La YO60 ....... 7 C2
Malton Rd
  Huntington YO32 .... 47 C2
  York YO31 ........... 52 B4
Malton Way YO30 .... 45 B1
Malt Shoval Ct YO1 .. 65 C2
Malvern Ave YO26 ... 49 C2
Malvern Cl YO32 ..... 42 B2
Mancroft **20** YO32 .. 11 A1
Manley Cl YO32 ...... 41 C1
Manor Beeches The **3**
  YO19 ............... 23 A4
Manor CE Sec Sch
  YO26 ............... 49 B4
Manor Cl YO26 ....... 16 A1
Manor Ct **8** YO32 ... 42 B3
Manor Dr **2** YO19 .. 23 A4
Manor Dr N YO26 .... 49 C1
Manor Dr S YO26 .... 49 C1
Manor Farm Cl **1**
  YO23 ............... 26 C2
Manor Garth YO32 ... 10 C1
Manor Heath YO23 .. 26 C3
Manor La YO30 ...... 44 C3
Manor La YO10 ...... 45 A3
Manor Pk Gr **2**
  YO30 ............... 45 A3
Manor Pk Rd YO30 .. 45 A3
Manor Way YO30 .... 45 A3
Mansfield St YO31 ... 64 C3
Maple Ave YO23 ..... 27 C3
Maple Ct
  Wheldrake YO19 ..... 29 C1
  York YO10 ........... 62 A3
Maple Gr YO10 ...... 56 C2
Maplehurst Ave
  YO31 ............... 51 C4
Maplewood Paddock **2**
  YO24 ............... 54 B2
March St YO31 ....... 64 C4
Margaret Philipson Ct
  YO10 ............... 65 C3
Margaret St YO10 .... 65 C1
Marjorie Waite Ct
  YO30 ............... 51 A4
Market St YO1 ....... 65 B2
Markham Cres YO31 . 64 B4
Markham St YO31 ... 64 B4
Marlborough Cl
  YO30 ............... 44 C4
Marlborough Gr
  YO10 ............... 56 C3
Marlborough Villas
  YO10 ............... 56 C3
Marmiam Dr **2** YO32 17 C3
Marquis Ct YO26 .... 49 C2
Marston Ave YO26 .. 54 A4
Marston Cres YO26 .. 54 A4
Marten Cl **2** YO30 .. 45 C1
Martin Cheeseman Ct
  **8** YO24 ......... 54 B1
Martins Ct YO30 .... 50 C2
Marygate YO30 ...... 64 A3
Marygate La YO30 ... 64 A3
Mask La YO41 ........ 24 C1
Mattison Way YO24 . 55 A3
Mayfield Gr YO24 .... 55 A4
Maypole Gr **8** YO19 27 C1
Maythorn Rd YO31 .. 47 A3
Maythorpe YO23 ..... 20 B3
Meadlands YO31 ..... 53 A3
Meadowbeck Cl
  YO10 ............... 53 A1
Meadow Ct **3** YO24 . 55 A1
Meadowfields Dr
  YO31 ............... 46 C3
Meadow La **21** YO32 . 11 A1

Meadows The **2**
  YO30 ............... 39 A2
Meadow Way
  Heworth YO31 ....... 52 B4
  Huntington YO32 .... 42 B1
Meam Cl YO10 ...... 53 C1
Melander Cl YO30 ... 49 A1
Melander Gdns **5**
  YO30 ............... 41 C4
Melbourne St YO10 .. 56 C3
Melcombe Ave **11**
  YO32 ............... 11 C4
Melrose Cl **1** YO32 . 12 A1
Melrosegate YO31 ... 52 B2
Melton Ave YO30 .... 45 B1
Melton Dr
  **7** Bishopthorpe
  YO23 ............... 27 C3
  York YO30 ........... 45 B1
Melwood Gr YO26 ... 49 A2
Menchester Way YO31 53 B2
Mendip Cl **2** YO32 .. 42 B2
Merchant Adventurers
  Hall* YO1 .......... 65 C2
Merchantgate YO1 ... 65 C2
Merchants Ct YO31 .. 52 A2
Merchant Way YO23 . 26 C3
Merlin Covert **4**
  YO31 ............... 53 B2
Metcalfe La YO19 .... 53 B4
Micklegate YO1 ...... 65 A2
Micklegate Bar Mus *
  YO1 ............... 65 A1
Middle Banks **24**
  YO32 ............... 11 A2
Middlecroft Dr YO32 . 11 A4
Middlecroft Gr **2**
  YO32 ............... 12 A4
Middleham Ave
  YO31 ............... 47 A1
MIDDLETHORPE .... 61 A3
Middlethorpe Dr
  YO23 ............... 60 B4
Middlethorpe Gr
  YO24 ............... 60 B4
Middleton Rd YO24 .. 54 B3
Middlewood Cl YO23 . 20 B3
Midgley Cl **6** YO41 . 19 C3
Midway Ave **5** YO26 . 16 C2
Mildred Gr **2** YO24 . 55 B3
Milestone Ave YO23 . 28 A4
Milford Mews **7**
  YO32 ............... 41 C4
Milford Way **6** YO32 41 C4
Millers Croft **6** YO23 28 A4
Millfield Ave YO10 ... 57 B4
Millfield Ct YO32 .... 42 B3
Millfield Gdns YO26 . 16 C2
Millfield La
  Nether Poppleton
  YO26 ............... 44 A1
  Poppleton YO26 ..... 16 C2
York YO10 .......... 57 C4
Millfield Rd YO23 .... 56 A3
Millgates YO26 ...... 49 B3
Mill Hill YO19 ....... 36 A3
Mill Hill Dr YO32 .... 42 B1
Mill La
  Acaster Malbis YO23 . 27 B1
  Askham Richard YO23 25 C3
  Haxby YO32 ......... 10 C4
  Hessay YO23 ........ 32 A3
  York YO31 ........... 52 A3
Mill Mount YO24 .... 55 C4
Mill Mount Ct YO24 . 55 C4
Mill St YO1 .......... 65 C1
Millthorpe Sec Sch
  YO23 ............... 56 A3
Milner St YO24 ...... 54 C4
Milson Gr YO10 ..... 57 C4
Milton Carr **8** YO30 45 B2
Milton St YO10 ...... 56 C3
Minchin Cl **3** YO30 . 46 A2
Minster Ave YO31 ... 47 B3
Minster Cl
  **3** Haxby YO32 .... 11 A1
  York YO31 ........... 64 B3
Minster Ct YO31 ..... 64 B3
Minster Sch The YO1 64 B3
Minster View **2**
  YO32 ............... 11 A1
Minster Yd YO1 ..... 64 B3
Minter Cl **2** YO32 .. 42 B3
Mistral Ct YO1 ...... 47 A1
Mitchell La YO41 .... 19 C1
Mitchell Way YO30 .. 45 A4
Mitchel's La YO10 ... 57 B1
Mitredale **4** YO32 .. 11 A1
Moat Field YO10 .... 53 C1
Moatside Ct YO1 .... 64 A3
Moins Ct YO10 ...... 53 C1
Moiser Cl YO32 ..... 42 B3
Monarch Way YO26 . 49 C3
Monk Ave YO31 ..... 52 B4
Monk Bar Ct YO31 .. 64 C3
Monk Bar & Richard III
  Mus * YO31 ........ 64 C3
Monkbridge Ct YO31 64 C3
Monkgate YO31 ..... 64 C3

Monkgate Cloisters
  YO31 ............... 64 C3
Monks Cross Dr
  YO32 ............... 47 C4
Monks Cross Link
  YO32 ............... 43 A1
Monks Cross Sh Pk
  YO32 ............... 48 A4
Monkton Rd **5** YO31 47 B2
Montague Rd **14**
  YO23 ............... 27 C3
Montague St YO23 .. 56 B2
Montague Wlk **6**
  YO23 ............... 27 C3
Montrose Ave YO31 . 46 C1
Moor Cl YO19 ....... 30 B1
Moorcroft Rd YO24 . 59 C4
Moore Ave YO10 .... 53 A1
Moorgarth Ave **10**
  YO24 ............... 55 B3
Moorgate YO24 ..... 54 C4
Moor Gr YO24 ...... 55 A1
Moor La
  Bilbrough LS24 ...... 25 A2
  Bishopthorpe YO23 .. 27 B2
  Copmanthorpe YO23 . 26 C2
  Earswick YO32 ...... 12 A2
  Haxby YO32 ......... 10 C4
  Murton YO19 ........ 17 C1
  Naburn YO19 ........ 27 C1
  Newton-on-Ouse YO30 .8 B4
  Rufforth YO23 ....... 21 A3
  Skelton YO30 ........ 39 C3
  Stensall YO32 ....... 12 A4
  Thornton-le-Clay YO60 .7 B3
  York YO24 ........... 59 B3
Moorland Garth **2**
  YO32 ............... 11 C4
Moorland Rd YO10 .. 56 C2
Moorland Rd YO10 .. 56 C1
Moorlands YO32 .... 10 A2
Moorlands Cl YO10 .. 53 B1
Moorlands Fields
  YO10 ............... 57 A1
Moorlands La
  Skelton YO30 ....... 39 B3
  **1** Tollerton YO61 .. 2 A4
Moorlands Nature
  Reserve* YO32 ..... 10 A2
Moor Rd YO41 ...... 19 C3
Moor Way YO32 .... 42 C1
Morcar Rd YO41 .... 19 C2
Morehall Cl YO30 ... 45 B2
Morell Cl YO24 ..... 54 A1
Morrell Ave YO10 ... 57 C3
Morritt Cl **3** YO31 .. 47 B1
Moss St YO24 ....... 65 A1
Mount Ephraim **6**
  YO24 ............... 55 C4
Mount Par YO24 .... 55 C4
Mount Sch The YO24 55 C4
Mount Terr YO24 .... 55 C4
Mount The YO24 .... 65 A1
Mount Vale YO24 ... 55 C3
Mount Vale Dr YO24 55 C3
Mowbray Dr YO30 .. 49 B1
Muirfield Way **6**
  YO26 ............... 49 A2
Mulberry Ct YO32 .. 42 A3
Mulberry Dr **7** YO32 11 A2
Mulwith Cl YO31 .... 52 C3
Muncastergate YO31 52 A4
Murray St YO24 ..... 55 B4
Murrough Wilson Pl **3**
  YO31 ............... 52 A4
MURTON ............ 22 C4
Murton Garth YO19 . 22 B4
Murton La YO19 .... 22 C4
Murton Way YO19 .. 22 C1
Museum St YO1 ..... 65 B2

## N

NABURN ............ 27 C1
Naburn CE Prim Sch
  YO19 ............... 27 C1
Naburn La
  Deighton YO19 ...... 35 C4
  Fulford YO19 ........ 61 C1
Naburn Pk Mews
  YO19 ............... 28 A1
Nairn Cl **3** YO24 .. 59 B3
Nalton Cl **16** YO23 . 26 C2
Narrow La YO42 ..... 38 C4
National Ctr for Early
  Music* YO1 ........ 65 C2
National Rly Mus *
  YO26 ............... 50 C1
Navigation Rd YO1 .. 65 C2
Nelson's La YO24 ... 55 B2
Nelson St YO31 ..... 64 C4
Nessgate YO1 ....... 65 B2
NETHER POPPLETON
  .................... 16 C2
Nether Way **20** YO26 16 B2
Netherwindings **7**
  YO32 ............... 11 B2

Netherwoods **6** YO32 6 A1
Neville Dr **8** YO23 . 27 C3
Neville St YO31 ..... 64 C4
Neville Terr YO31 ... 64 C4
Nevinson Gr YO10 .. 57 A1
New Ave YO24 ...... 59 A4
Newborough St
  YO30 ............... 64 A4
Newbury Ave YO24 . 54 C2
Newby Terr YO31 ... 51 B4
Newdale **3** YO32 .. 11 B2
NEW EARSWICK ... 46 C4
New Earswick Prim Sch
  YO32 ............... 41 C1
New Earswick Sports
  Club YO32 ......... 46 C4
New Forge Ct **15**
  YO10 ............... 11 B2
Newgate YO1 ....... 65 B2
Newgate Ct YO1 .... 65 B2
New La
  Bishopthorpe YO23 .. 60 C1
  Holgate YO24 ....... 54 C4
  Huntington YO32 .... 47 B2
  Lillings Ambo YO60 .. 6 B4
  Long Marston YO23 . 25 A4
  Stensall YO32 ........ 6 A1
Newland Pk Cl YO10 57 B4
Newland Pk Dr YO10 57 B4
Newlands Dr YO26 .. 49 A3
Newlands La YO26 .. 15 A3
Newlands Rd YO23 .. 60 B1
New Rd
  Appleton Roebuck
  YO23 ............... 33 A2
  Beningbrough YO30 .. 8 B3
  Hessay YO23 ........ 15 A2
  Lillings Ambo YO60 .. 6 B4
  Wheldrake YO19 ..... 36 B4
New St YO1 ......... 65 B2
Newton House Ct
  YO61 ............... 3 A2
NEWTON-ON-OUSE . 8 A3
Newton Pk YO30 .... 8 A4
Newton Rd YO61 .... 2 A4
Newton Terr YO1 ... 65 B1
New Wlk Terr YO10 . 65 C1
Nicholas Gdns YO10 57 B4
Nicholas St YO10 ... 57 B4
Nidd Cl YO24 ....... 44 A1
Nidd Gr YO24 ...... 55 A1
Nigel Gr **7** YO24 .. 55 A1
Nightingale Cl YO32 47 A2
Ninth Ave YO31 .... 52 B3
Norfolk St YO23 .... 56 B3
Norman Dr **1** YO26 . 49 A3
Norman St **5** YO10 . 57 C4
Norseway **2** YO41 . 19 C2
Northcote Ave YO10 . 57 A1
Northcroft **5** YO32 . 11 B2
North Eastern Terr
  YO31 ............... 52 A3
Northern Backlight
  Theatre YO31 ...... 64 C4
North Field Ave YO23 33 B2
North Field Cl YO23 . 33 B2
North Field La
  Askham Bryan YO23 . 26 B4
  Upper Poppleton YO26 21 B4
Northfields **8** YO32 . 11 B2
Northfield Sch YO26 . 49 C2
Northfield Terr YO31 . 55 A1
North Field Way
  YO23 ............... 33 B2
Northgate La YO41 .. 18 C4
North Grange Ct
  YO30 ............... 64 A4
North La
  Dringhouses YO24 ... 55 A1
  Huntington YO32 .... 42 B2
  Wheldrake YO19 ..... 37 B4
Northlands Ave **1**
  YO32 ............... 11 B2
Northminster Bsns Pk
  YO26 ............... 50 B4
North Moor Gdns
  YO32 ............... 42 B2
North Moor Rd **2** YO32 42 B2
Northolme Dr YO30 . 45 A2
North Parade YO30 . 64 A3
North St YO1 ........ 65 B2
Norway Dr YO10 ... 56 C1
Nunmill St YO23 .... 56 B3
Nun Monkton
  Foundation Prim Sch
  YO26 ............... 9 C2
NUNTHORPE ....... 56 A1
Nunthorpe Ave YO23 56 B3
Nunthorpe Cres
  YO23 ............... 56 A2
Nunthorpe Gr YO23 . 56 A2
Nunthorpe Rd YO23 . 65 A1
Nursery Cl **1** YO10 . 57 B2
Nursery Dr YO24 ... 55 A3
Nursery Gdns YO10 . 58 B4
Nursery Rd **4** YO26 . 16 C2

## O

Oak Busk La YO60 .... 7 B2
Oakdale Rd YO30 ... 45 B3
Oak Glade **6** YO31 . 53 B2
Oakhill Cres **3** YO32 11 C3
Oakland Ave YO31 .. 52 C4
Oakland Dr YO31 ... 52 C4
Oaklands **5** YO32 .. 42 A3
Oaklands Sec Sch
  YO24 ............... 54 B3
Oaklands Sports Ctr
  YO24 ............... 54 B3
Oak Rise **4** YO26 .. 54 B4
Oak St **3** YO26 .... 50 A2
Oak Tree Cl YO32 ... 42 A3
Oak Tree Ct YO32 .. 41 B4
Oak Tree Gr **5** YO32 46 C4
Oak Tree La YO19 .. 35 C4
Oak Tree Way **10**
  YO32 ............... 12 A4
Oakville St YO31 .... 51 C4
Ogleforth YO1 ....... 64 B3
Old Coppice **14** YO32 11 B2
Old Dike Lands **34**
  YO32 ............... 11 A1
Old Hall La YO41 ... 24 C1
Old Lane Ct LS24 ... 33 A4
Oldman Ct YO24 .... 54 B1
Old Moor La YO24 .. 60 A4
Old Orchard YO32 .. 11 A4
Old Orchard The
  Fulford YO10 ....... 62 A4
  Shipton YO30 ........ 9 B2
Old Rd YO23 ........ 33 A2
Old St The LS24 .... 33 A4
Old Village The YO32 42 A3
Olympian Ct YO10 .. 52 B1
Orchard Cl
  Appleton Roebuck
  YO23 ............... 33 B2
  York YO24 ........... 55 A2
Orchard Cotts **4**
  YO35 ............... 23 B4
Orchard Garth YO23 26 C2
Orchard Gdns YO31 47 A3
Orchard Paddock
  **6** Haxby YO32 .... 11 A1
  **34** Haxby YO32 ... 11 A1
Orchard Rd **7** YO16 56 C2
Orchard The **18** YO25 27 C3
Orchard The YO10 .. 57 B1
Orchard View **3**
  YO30 ............... 39 A2
Orchard Way
  **1** Stensall YO32 .. 12 A4
  York YO31 ........... 52 C3
Ordnance La YO10 .. 56 C2
Oriel Gr YO30 ....... 45 C1
Orrin Cl YO30 ...... 59 B4
OSBALDWICK ...... 53 B1
Osbaldwick La YO10 . 53 A2
Osbaldwick Link Rd
  YO10 ............... 53 B1
Osbaldwick Prim Sch
  YO10 ............... 53 B1
Osbaldwick Village
  YO10 ............... 53 B1
Osbourne Dr **4**
  YO24 ............... 45 A4
Osmington Gdns **10**
  YO32 ............... 11 B2
Osprey Cl **3** YO24 . 59 A1
Ostler's Cl **7** YO23 . 27 A3
Ostman Rd YO32 ... 49 B2
Otterwood Bank **6**
  YO24 ............... 54 A2
Otterwood La YO24 . 54 A2
Otterwood Paddock
  YO24 ............... 11 B3
Our Ladys RC Prim Sch
  YO24 ............... 54 C2
Ouse Acres YO26 ... 49 C3
Ouseburn Ave YO26 49 B3
Ousecliffe Gdns
  YO30 ............... 50 C3
Ouse Lea YO30 ..... 50 C4
Outgang La YO19 ... 35 C4
Overdale Ct YO24 .. 54 B1
OVERTON .......... 16 B3
Overton Rd YO30 ... 16 A4
Ovington Terr YO23 . 56 A3
Owlwood Cl **4** YO19 23 A4
Owlwood La **5** YO19 23 A4
Owston Ave **3** YO10 56 C1
Ox Calder Cl **2** YO19 23 B4
Ox Carr La YO32 ... 12 A3
Ox Cl YO41 ......... 19 C3
Oxford St **5** YO24 .. 55 C4

## P

Paddock Cl
  Askham Richard
  YO23 ............... 25 C4

Paddock Cl continued
  **13** Copmanthorpe
  YO23 ............... 26 C2
Paddock The YO26 .. 49 B3
Paddock Way YO26 . 49 B3
Palmer La YO1 ...... 65 C2
Palmes Cl YO19 .... 28 A1
Panman La YO19 ... 18 B1
Parade Ct YO31 .... 52 B3
Paragon St YO10 ... 65 C1
Park Ave YO23 ..... 41 C2
Park Cl YO30 ....... 39 A1
Park Cres YO31 .... 64 C4
Parker Ave YO26 ... 54 A3
Park Est **36** YO32 .. 11 A1
Park Gate YO31 ...... 6 A1
Park Gr YO31 ....... 64 C4
Park Gr Sch YO31 .. 64 C4
Park La YO19 ....... 55 B4
Parkland Way **5**
  YO32 ............... 11 A1
Park Lodge YO32 ... 41 C1
Park Pl YO31 ....... 64 C4
Parkside Cl YO24 ... 55 A4
Parkside Commercial
  Ctr YO23 .......... 65 C1
Park St YO24 ....... 65 A1
Park Terr YO31 ..... 41 C2
Parliament St YO1 .. 65 B2
Parsons La YO26 ... 16 A2
Paston Wlk YO25 .. 65 B1
Pasture Cl
  Skelton YO30 ....... 39 A2
  **2** Stensall YO32 .. 12 A3
Pasture Farm Cl
  YO10 ............... 61 C3
Pasture La YO41 ... 48 A1
Pastures The **4**
  YO23 ............... 55 A1
Pately Pl **1** YO26 .. 49 C1
Patrick Pool YO1 ... 65 B2
Patterdale Dr YO30 . 45 A2
Pavement YO1 ..... 65 B2
Paver La YO1 ...... 65 C2
Pear Tree Ave **8**
  YO26 ............... 16 B2
Pear Tree Cl YO32 . 42 B1
Peartree Ct YO1 .... 64 C3
Peasholme Gn YO1 . 65 B1
Peckitt St YO1 ...... 65 B1
Peel Cl YO10 ....... 57 C2
Peel St YO1 ......... 65 B1
Pelham Pl **15** YO32 . 11 C4
Pembroke St YO30 . 51 A4
Penley's Gr St YO31 . 64 C4
Pennine Cl YO32 ... 42 B1
Penny La YO31 .... 64 C3
Pentire Cl **11** YO10 . 45 C2
Pentland Dr YO32 .. 47 A4
Penyghent Ave YO31 52 C2
Peppercorn Cl **6**
  YO24 ............... 50 A1
Percy's La YO1 ..... 65 C2
Percy St YO31 ...... 64 B3
Petercroft Cl **5**
  YO19 ............... 23 B4
Petercroft La YO19 . 23 B4
Peter Hill Dr YO30 . 45 C1
Peter La YO1 ....... 65 B2
Petersway YO30 .... 64 A3
Pheasant Dr **5** YO24 54 A1
Philadelphia Terr **2**
  YO23 ............... 56 A3
Phoenix Bvd YO26 . 50 C1
Picadilly Ct YO1 .... 65 C2
Piccadilly YO1 ...... 65 C2
Pike Hills Mount
  YO23 ............... 26 C3
Pilgrim St YO31 .... 64 B4
Pinelands **4** YO32 . 41 C4
Pinelands Way YO10 58 B4
Pinewood Gr **6**
  YO31 ............... 47 A3
Pinewood Hill YO10 58 B4
Pinfold Ct **3** YO30 . 50 C4
Pinsent Ct YO31 ... 47 A1
Plantation Dr YO26 . 49 B3
Plantation Gr YO26 . 49 B3
Plantation Way **28**
  YO32 ............... 11 A2
Ploughlands **3** YO32 41 B4
Ploughman's Cl **4**
  YO23 ............... 27 A3
Ploughman's La
  YO23 ............... 41 B4
Plumer Ave YO31 .. 52 C2
Pollard Ct YO32 ... 47 A4
Poplar Gr YO32 .... 47 A4
Poplar St YO26 .... 50 A2
Poppleton Hall Gdn
  YO26 ............... 16 C3
Poppleton Rd YO26 . 54 B4
Poppleton Rd Prim Sch
  YO26 ............... 50 A2
Poppleton Sta YO26 16 B1
Portal Rd YO26 .... 49 A3

Portisham Pl 12

YO32 . . . . . . . . . . . 11 C4
Portland St YO31 . . . . 64 B4
Postern Cl YO23 . . . . . 65 B1
Postern La YO42 . . . . . 38 C3
Potters Dr 22 YO26 . . 26 C3
Pottery La YO31 . . . . . 52 A4
Precentor's Ct YO31 . 64 B3
Prestwick Ct YO26 . . . 49 A2
Price's La YO23 . . . . . . 65 B1
Priest La YO19 . . . . . . 23 B2
Princess Dr YO26 . . . . 49 C3
Princess Rd YO32 . . . . 12 A4
Prior's Wlk YO26 . . . . . 49 C3
Priory St YO1 . . . . . . . 65 A1
Priory Wood Way

YO31 . . . . . . . . . . . 47 B3
Prospect Terr

Fulford YO10 . . . . . . 61 C3
York YO1 . . . . . . . . . 65 B1
Pulleyn Cl 3 YO32 . . 6 B1
Pulleyn Dr YO24 . . . . . 55 B2
Purey Cust Nuffield

Hospl The YO31 . . . 64 B3

**Q**

Quaker Gn 1 YO24 . . 59 B4
Quant Mews YO10 . . . 58 A4
Queen Annes Rd

YO30 . . . . . . . . . . . 64 A3
Queen Margaret's Sch

YO19 . . . . . . . . . . . 35 C2
Queen's Ct YO1 . . . . . . 65 B1
Queens Staith Mews

YO1 . . . . . . . . . . . . 65 B1
Queen's Staith Rd

YO1 . . . . . . . . . . . . 65 B2
Queen St YO24 . . . . . . 65 A2
Queenswood Gr

YO24 . . . . . . . . . . . 54 C3
Queen Victoria St

YO23 . . . . . . . . . . . 56 A2

**R**

Racecourse Rd YO23 56 B1
Railway Terr YO24 . . . 50 C1
Railway View YO24 . . 55 A2
Rainsborough Way 3

YO30 . . . . . . . . . . . 45 C1
Raker Cl YO19 . . . . . . . 37 B4
Ralph Butterfield Prim

Sch YO32 . . . . . . . . 11 B2
Rampart The YO23 . . . 32 C1
Ramsay Cl YO31 . . . . . 64 C4
Ratcliffe Ct YO30 . . . . 39 B2
Ratcliffe St YO30 . . . . 51 A4
Raven Gr YO26 . . . . . . 49 B1
RAWCLIFFE . . . . . . . . 45 A3
Rawcliffe Ave YO30 . . 45 A3
Rawcliffe Croft YO30 44 C3
Rawcliffe Dr YO30 . . . 45 B1
Rawcliffe Inf Sch

YO30 . . . . . . . . . . . 45 A2
Rawcliffe La YO30 . . . . 45 A2
Rawcliffe Landing

YO30 . . . . . . . . . . . 44 B4
Rawcliffe Village

YO30 . . . . . . . . . . . 45 A4
Rawcliffe Way YO30 . . 45 A3
Rawdon Ave YO10 . . . 52 B1
Rectory Cl YO23 . . . . . 32 C1
Rectory Gdns YO42 . . 56 A2
Redbarn Dr YO10 . . . . 53 C1
Redcap La YO42 . . . . . 38 B2
Redcoat Way 1

YO24 . . . . . . . . . . . 54 A1
Redeness St YO1 . . . . 52 A2
Redgrave Cl 4 YO31 47 A1
Redhill Field La

YO23 . . . . . . . . . . . 25 C2
Redman Cl YO10 . . . . . 56 B1
Redmayne Sq YO32 . . 6 A1
Redmires Cl YO30 . . . 45 A2
Redthorn Dr YO31 . . . 47 B2
Red Twr★ YO1 . . . . . . 52 A1
Redwood Dr 3 YO32 11 A2
Reeves The YO24 . . . . 54 B2
Regency Mews 2

YO24 . . . . . . . . . . . 55 B1
Regents Ct 14 YO30 50 B2
Regent St YO10 . . . . . 52 A1
Regimental Mus★

YO1 . . . . . . . . . . . . 65 B1
Reginald Gr YO23 . . . . 56 B2
Reighton Ave YO31 . . 45 B1
Reighton Dr 10 YO30 45 B1
Renshaw Gdns 6

YO26 . . . . . . . . . . . 50 A4
Retreat Hospl The

YO10 . . . . . . . . . . . 57 B3
Reygate Gr 8 YO23 . 26 C2
Ribstone Gr YO31 . . . . 53 A3
Rice La YO60 . . . . . . . . .7 B3

Richardson St YO23 . . 56 B3
Richmond St YO31 . . . 52 A2
Ridgeway YO26 . . . . . . 54 A4
Ringstone Rd

Bishopthorpe YO23 . 61 A2
York YO30 . . . . . . . . 45 B3
Ripley Gr 3 YO32 . . . . 11 A2
Risewood YO41 . . . . . . 19 A3
Rishworth Gr YO30 . . 45 B1
Rivelin Way YO30 . . . . 45 C1
Riversdale 17 YO32 . . 11 B2
Riverside Cl 11 YO41 31 B3
Riverside Cres YO32 . . 42 B3
Riverside Gdns

2 Elvington YO41 . . 27 C3
2 Poppleton YO26 . . 16 B2
Riverside Wlk

1 Poppleton YO26 . . 16 B2
5 Strensall YO32 . . . 11 C4
River St YO23 . . . . . . . 65 B1
Riversvale Dr YO26 . . 54 A4
Robert Wilkinson Prim

Sch YO32 . . . . . . . . 11 C4
Robin Gr 6 YO24 . . . . 55 B4
Robinson Ct YO41 . . . . 65 C2
Robinson Dr YO24 . . . 54 A3
Roche Ave YO31 . . . . . 47 A2
Rockingham Ave

YO31 . . . . . . . . . . . 52 C2
Rogers Ct YO24 . . . . . . 54 B1
Roland Ct YO32 . . . . . . 47 A4
Rolston Ave 1 YO31 . 47 A3
Roman Ave N 17

YO41 . . . . . . . . . . . 19 C2
Roman Ave S YO41 . . . 19 C2
Roman Camps★

YO41 . . . . . . . . . . . 19 C2
Ropers Ct 2 YO23 . . 27 A3
Ropewalk The YO31 . . 52 A2
Roseberry Gr YO30 . . 45 B4
Roseberry St YO26 . . . 50 B4
Rosecomb Way 6

YO30 . . . . . . . . . . . 41 C4
Rosecroft Way YO30 . 45 A3
Rosedale Ave YO30 . . 49 B1
Rosedale St YO10 . . . . 56 C3
Rosemary Ct YO1 . . . . 65 C2
Rosemary Pl YO1 . . . . 65 C2
Rose St YO31 . . . . . . . . 51 B4
Rose Tree Gr YO32 . . . 11 C4
Rosslyn St 1 YO30 . . 50 C3
Rougier St YO1 . . . . . . 65 A2
Round Hill Link YO30 45 B3
Rowan Ave YO31 . . . . . 52 A4
Rowan Pl YO30 . . . . . . 41 C1
Rowley Ct 2 YO32 . . . 42 B4
Rowmans The YO30 . . 39 A4
Rowntree Ave YO30 . . 46 B1
Royal Chase YO24 . . . 55 B1
Ruby St 3 YO10 . . . . . 56 A2
Rudcar La YO19 . . . . . . 36 C4
Ruddings YO31 . . . . . . 30 C1
Ruddings Cl 18 YO32 11 A1
Ruffhams Cl YO19 . . . 38 A1
RUFFORTH . . . . . . . . . 20 B3
Rufforth Prim Sch

YO23 . . . . . . . . . . . 20 B3
Runswick Ave YO26 . . 49 A1
Rushwood Cl 6

YO32 . . . . . . . . . . . 11 A2
Russell Dr YO30 . . . . . 45 A1
Russell St YO23 . . . . . . 56 A3
Russet Dr YO31 . . . . . . 53 A2
Rutland Cl 7 YO23 . . 26 C3
Ryburn Cl YO30 . . . . . . 45 A1
Rydal Ave YO31 . . . . . . 52 C3
Rye Cl 11 YO32 . . . . . . 11 A1
Ryecroft 7 YO32 . . . . 11 C3
Ryecroft Ave YO26 . . 59 B4
Ryecroft Cl YO31 . . . . 48 B1
Ryehill Cl YO32 . . . . . . 41 C2
Ryemoor Rd 22 YO32 11 A1
Rylatt Cl YO23 . . . . . . . 65 B1

**S**

Sadberge Ct YO10 . . . 58 B4
Saddlers Cl

18 Copmanthorpe

YO23 . . . . . . . . . . . 26 C3
Huntington YO32 . . 47 B3
Sails Dr YO10 . . . . . . . 58 B4
St Aelreds Ct YO31 . . 52 B1
St Aelreds RC Prim Sch

YO31 . . . . . . . . . . . 53 A2
St Andrewgate YO1 . . 65 B2
St Andrew Pl YO1 . . . . 65 C2
St Ann Ct YO10 . . . . . . 56 C3
St Ann's Ct YO10 . . . . 56 C3
St Aubyn's Pl YO24 . . 55 C3
St Barnabas' CE Prim

Sch YO26 . . . . . . . . 50 B2
St Barnabas Ct 13

YO26 . . . . . . . . . . . 50 B2
St Benedict Rd YO23 . 65 B1
St Bridget's Ct YO23 . 65 B1

St Catherines YO30 . . 39 C3
St Catherines Cl

YO30 . . . . . . . . . . . 39 B2
St Catherines Pl

YO30 . . . . . . . . . . . 55 C4
St Chads Wharf YO23 56 B1
St Clement's Gr YO23 56 B3
St Denys' Rd YO1 . . . . 65 C2
St Edmunds YO41 . . . . 19 C3
St Edward's Ct YO24 . 55 B1
St George's Pl YO24 . . 55 B3
St George's RC Prim

Sch YO10 . . . . . . . . 56 C3
St Giles Ct YO31 . . . . . 64 B3
St Giles Rd YO30 . . . . 39 A2
St Giles Way YO30 . . . 26 C2
St Gregory's Mews

YO1 . . . . . . . . . . . . 65 A2
St Helen's Rd 5

YO24 . . . . . . . . . . . 55 A1
St Helen's Rise YO19 37 C4
St Helen's Sq YO1 . . . 65 B2
St Hildas Mews YO10 53 A1
St James Cl YO30 . . . . 45 A4
St James Mount

YO24 . . . . . . . . . . . 55 C3
St James Pl 5 YO24 . 54 C2
St John's Cres YO31 . . 64 C4
St John's Rd YO41 . . . 19 C3
St John St YO31 . . . . . 64 B3
St Lawrences CE Prim

Sch YO10 . . . . . . . . 57 A4
St Leonard's Pl YO30 64 B3
St Luke's Gr YO30 . . . 51 A4
St Margaret's Terr

YO31 . . . . . . . . . . . 52 A1
St Mark's Gr YO30 . . . 45 A3
St Martin's La YO1 . . . 65 A2
St Mary's YO30 . . . . . . 63 A4
St Marys CE Prim Sch

YO30 . . . . . . . . . . . 25 C4
St Mary's Cl YO42 . . . 38 B2
St Mary's Cl

15 Haxby YO32 . . . . 11 A2
Strensall YO32 . . . . . 11 C4
St Mary's Ct YO24 . . . 55 A1
St Mary's Gr YO30 . . . 51 B1
St Mary's La YO23 . . . 64 B3
St Mary's Mus★ YO1 65 B2
St Mary's Terr YO30 . 64 B3
St Matthew's Cl 4

YO19 . . . . . . . . . . . 27 C1
St Maurice's Rd

YO31 . . . . . . . . . . . 65 B3
St Nicholas Ave

YO19 . . . . . . . . . . . 61 C1
St Nicholas Cl 4

YO23 . . . . . . . . . . . 26 C3
St Nicholas Cres 2

YO23 . . . . . . . . . . . 26 C3
St Nicholas Croft

YO23 . . . . . . . . . . . 26 A4
St Nicholas Fields

Nature Reserve★

YO10 . . . . . . . . . . . 52 B1
St Nicholas Pl 1

YO10 . . . . . . . . . . . 57 B4
St Nicholas Rd 3

YO10 . . . . . . . . . . . 57 B4
St Nicholas Way 2

YO32 . . . . . . . . . . . 11 A2
St Olave's Rd YO30 . . 64 A4
St Olave's Sch YO30 . 64 A4
St Oswald's CE Prim

Sch YO10 . . . . . . . . 62 A4
St Oswalds Ct YO10 . . 62 A4
St Oswald's Rd YO10 62 A4
St Paul's CE Prim Sch

YO24 . . . . . . . . . . . 55 C4
St Pauls Mews YO24 . 55 C4
St Paul's Sq 3 YO24 . 55 C4
St Paul's Sq YO24 . . . 55 C4
St Paul's Terr YO24 . . 50 C1
St Peters Cl YO26 . . . 21 C4
St Peter's Gr YO30 . . . 64 A4
St Peter's Sch YO30 . 64 A4
St Philip's Gr YO30 . . 45 C1
St Saviourgate YO1 . . 65 C2
St Saviour's Pl YO1 . . 65 C2
St Saviour's Sch YO1 65 C2
St Stephens Mews

YO30 . . . . . . . . . . . 45 C3
St Stephen's Rd YO24 54 B1
St Stephen's Sq YO24 54 B2
St Swithin's Wlk

YO26 . . . . . . . . . . . 50 A1
St Thomas' Pl YO31 . . 64 B4
St Thomas's Cl 2

YO31 . . . . . . . . . . . 53 B1
St Wilfrid's RC Prim

Sch YO31 . . . . . . . . 64 A4
St Wilfrid's Ct 7

YO32 . . . . . . . . . . . 12 A3
St Wilfrid's Cres 8

YO32 . . . . . . . . . . . 42 B4
St Wilfrid's Rd 8

YO32 . . . . . . . . . . . 42 B4

St Williams Coll

YO31 . . . . . . . . . . . 64 B3
St Wulstan Cl YO31 . . 64 A4
Salisbury Rd YO26 . . . 50 B2
Salisbury Terr YO26 . . 50 B2
Salmond Rd 1 YO24 . 54 A2
Sandacre Ct YO26 . . . 49 C2
Sandcroft Cl YO24 . . . 54 C1
Sandcroft Rd YO24 . . 54 C1
Sandholme 2 YO32 . 11 B2
SAND HUTTON . . . . . . 14 A2
Sand Hutton CE VC

Prim Sch YO41 . . . 14 A2
Sand Hutton La YO41 14 A2
Sandmartin Ct YO24 . 54 C1
Sandown Ct YO24 . . . 49 A1
Sandringham Cl

YO32 . . . . . . . . . . . 41 B4
Sandringham St

YO10 . . . . . . . . . . . 56 C3
Sandstock Rd YO31 . . 53 A4
Sandy Gap YO32 . . . . 41 B4
Sandy La

19 Haxby YO32 . . . . 11 A2
Stockton on the Forest

YO32 . . . . . . . . . . . 13 A1
Sandyland 23 YO32 . 11 A2
Sandyridge 9 YO26 . 16 B2
Sargent Ave YO23 . . . 60 B1
Saville Gr YO30 . . . . . . 51 A4
Sawyer's Cres 33

YO23 . . . . . . . . . . . 26 C3
Sawyers Wlk 9 YO19 23 B4
Saxford Way 10 YO32 10 C2
Saxon Cl YO30 . . . . . . . .9 B2
Saxon Pl YO31 . . . . . . . 52 A4
Saxon Rd YO41 . . . . . . 19 C3
Saxon Vale YO30 . . . . . .9 B2
Scafell Cl 4 YO30 . . . 45 C1
Scaife Gdns YO31 . . . . 51 B4
Scaife St YO31 . . . . . . 51 B4
Scarborough Terr

YO30 . . . . . . . . . . . 64 B4
Scarcroft Hill YO24 . . 56 A3
Scarcroft La YO23 . . . 65 A1
Scarcroft Prim Sch

YO23 . . . . . . . . . . . 65 A1
Scarcroft Rd YO23 . . . 56 A3
Scarcroft View YO23 . 65 A1
Scaudercroft 13

YO19 . . . . . . . . . . . 23 B4
Scawton Ave 1

YO31 . . . . . . . . . . . 47 A1
School 13 YO41 . . . . . 19 C3
School La

Askham Richard

YO23 . . . . . . . . . . . 25 C4
Bishopthorpe YO23 . 60 C1
11 Copmanthorpe

YO23 . . . . . . . . . . . 26 C2
Heslington YO10 . . . 58 A2
22 Poppleton YO26 . 16 B2
York YO10 . . . . . . . . 62 A4
School Sq YO24 . . . . . 54 A2
Scoreby La YO41 . . . . 19 A2
Scotchman La YO60 . . 7 C1
Scott Moncrieff Rd

YO32 . . . . . . . . . . . 12 A3
Scott St YO23 . . . . . . . 56 B3
Scriven Gr 8 YO31 . . 52 B1
Scrope Ave 4 YO31 . 52 A2
Seafire Cl YO30 . . . . . . 45 C4
Sealed La YO23 . . . . . . 25 B3
Seaton Cl YO10 . . . . . . 58 B3
Second Ave YO31 . . . . 52 B3
Sefton Ave YO31 . . . . 47 B1
Segrave Wlk 10 YO26 49 C2
Selby Rd YO19 . . . . . . . 63 C4
Seldon Rd YO26 . . . . . 50 A2
Seventh Ave YO31 . . . 52 B2
Severn Gn YO26 . . . . . 44 B1
Severus Ave YO30 . . . 55 A1
Severus St YO24 . . . . 54 C4
Seymour Gr YO31 . . . 53 A2
Shallowdale Gr 1

YO30 . . . . . . . . . . . 58 B4
Shambles YO1 . . . . . . 65 B2
Shaw's Terr YO24 . . . . 65 A1
Shelley Gr YO30 . . . . . 51 B1
Sheraton Dr

YO26 . . . . . . . . . . . 54 C1
Sherwood Gr

Huntington YO32 . . 47 B2
York YO26 . . . . . . . . 49 C1
Shilton Garth Cl 3

YO32 . . . . . . . . . . . 42 B4
SHIPTON . . . . . . . . . . . .9 B2
Shipton Low Rd YO30 .9 A2
Shipton Rd

Clifton YO30 . . . . . . 45 B1
Rawcliffe YO30 . . . . 44 C3
York YO30 . . . . . . . . 50 C4
Shipton Sch Inf Sch

YO30 . . . . . . . . . . . 51 A4
Shipton St 3 YO30 . . 51 A4
Shirbutt La YO19 . . . . 15 B1
Shirley Ave YO30 . . . . 50 B3
Shotel Cl YO30 . . . . . . 45 B1

Sills La YO30 . . . . . . . . .8 A3
Silverdale Ct YO24 . . . 59 C4
Silver St YO1 . . . . . . . . 65 B2
Sim Balk La YO24 . . . . 60 A2
Sirocco Ct YO31 . . . . . 46 C1
Sitwell Gr YO26 . . . . . 49 B1
Siwards How★ YO10 57 B1
Siward St YO10 . . . . . . 57 C4
Siward's Way YO10 . . 57 C3
Sixth Ave YO31 . . . . . . 52 A2
Skates La YO61 . . . . . . .4 A4
Skeldergate YO1 . . . . 65 B2
SKELTON . . . . . . . . . . 39 B3
Skelton Ct 3 YO30 . . 51 A4
Skelton La YO32 . . . . . 10 A1
Skelton Prim Sch

YO30 . . . . . . . . . . . 39 B2
Skewsby Gr YO31 . . . . 47 B2
Skiddaw YO24 . . . . . . . 59 B4
Skipwith Rd YO19 . . . 36 B3
Slessor Rd YO24 . . . . . 54 A2
Slingsby Gr YO24 . . . . 59 C3
Smales' St YO1 . . . . . . 65 B1
Smarty La YO19 . . . . . 22 C4
Smeaton Gr YO26 . . . . 49 B2
Smeaton Rd YO41 . . . 24 C4
Smith Cl YO10 . . . . . . 57 B1
Smithie Cl YO32 . . . . . 41 C2
Smith's La YO60 . . . . . . 6 C2
Snowdon Cl YO23 . . . 25 C4
Somerset Ct 6 YO30 55 A1
Somerset Rd YO41 . . 46 C1
South Back La YO61 . . .2 A3
SOUTH BANK . . . . . . . 56 A2
South Bank Ave

YO23 . . . . . . . . . . . 56 A2
South Down Rd 3

YO32 . . . . . . . . . . . 42 B2
South Espl YO1 . . . . . . 65 B1
Southfield Cl YO23 . . 20 C3
Southfield Cres 2

YO24 . . . . . . . . . . . 59 B4
Southfields Rd YO32 . 12 A4
Southlands 4 YO32 . 11 A2
Southlands YO19 . . . . 36 B3
Southlands Rd YO23 . 56 B2
Southmoor Rd YO19 . 37 B2
Southolme Dr 7

YO30 . . . . . . . . . . . 45 B2
South Parade YO23 . . 65 A1
South Ruddings La

YO19 . . . . . . . . . . . 37 B4
Southwood Rd YO41 . 31 B1
Sowerby Rd YO26 . . . 49 C1
Spalding Ave YO30 . . 51 A4
Speculation St YO1 . . 52 A1
Spencer St 3 YO23 . . 65 B1
Spen La YO26 . . . . . . . 20 C1
Spen La YO1 . . . . . . . . 65 B2
Spey Bank YO24 . . . . . 59 B3
Spindle Cl YO24 . . . . . 54 C1
Spinney The YO24 . . . 60 B4
Springbank Ave

YO19 . . . . . . . . . . . 23 A4
Springfield Rd YO26 . 64 C4
Springfield Rd 4

YO26 . . . . . . . . . . . 16 B2
Springfield Way

YO31 . . . . . . . . . . . 53 A4
Spring La YO10 . . . . . . 57 C2
Springwood YO32 . . . 41 B4
Spruce Cl YO32 . . . . . 46 C3
Spurr Ct YO10 . . . . . . 56 C3
Spurriergate YO1 . . . . 65 B2
Stabler Ct 15 YO30 . . 51 A4
Stablers Wlk YO32 . . 47 A2
Staindale Ct YO30 . . . 45 A3
Staithes Cl 4 YO26 . . 49 C2
Stamford Bridge Inf Sch

YO41 . . . . . . . . . . . 19 C3
Stamford Bridge Rd

YO19 . . . . . . . . . . . 23 A4
Stamford Bridge W

YO41 . . . . . . . . . . . 31 B1
Stamford St E 10

YO26 . . . . . . . . . . . 50 B2
Stamford St W 8

YO26 . . . . . . . . . . . 50 B2
Stanley Ave YO31 . . . 53 A4
Stanley St YO31 . . . . . 64 C4
Stanley Cres YO31 . . . 52 C2
Station Ave

New Earswick YO32 . 46 C4
York YO1 . . . . . . . . . 65 A2
Station La YO23 . . . . . . 9 A2
Station Rd

Copmanthorpe YO23 26 C2
Haxby YO32 . . . . . . . 11 B2
36 Poppleton YO26 . 16 B2
Riccall YO19 . . . . . . . 36 C1
York YO1 . . . . . . . . . 65 A2
Station Rise YO1 . . . . 65 A2
Station Sq 4 YO32 . . 12 A4
Steeple Ct 3 YO10 . . 12 C2
Steeton La YO1 . . . . . 65 A1
Stephenson Cl YO31 . 47 A2
Stephenson Way

YO26 . . . . . . . . . . . 50 B2

**Por–Tan 71**

Sterling Pk YO30 . . . . 45 C4
Sterne Ave YO31 . . . . 52 C2
Sterne Way YO61 . . . . .4 B4
Stewart La YO19 . . . . . 34 B1
Stirling Gr YO10 . . . . . 57 B1
Stirling Rd YO30 . . . . . 50 C4
Stockhill Cl 1 YO19 . . 23 A4
Stockholm Cl 1

YO31 . . . . . . . . . . . 56 C1
Stockton Hall YO32 . . 17 C4
Stockton La

Heworth YO32 . . . . . 48 C2
York YO32 . . . . . . . . 52 C4
STOCKTON ON THE

FOREST . . . . . . . . . 17 C4
Stockton on the Forest

Prim Sch YO32 . . . 17 C4
Stonebow The YO1 . . 65 C2
Stonegate YO1 . . . . . . 64 B3
Stonelands Ct 2

YO30 . . . . . . . . . . . 45 C2
Stone Riggs YO32 . . . 17 C3
Stones Cl YO24 . . . . . 55 A3
Stonethwaite 5

YO24 . . . . . . . . . . . 59 B4
Stoop Cl 25 YO32 . . . 11 A1
Stow Ct YO32 . . . . . . . 47 A4
Stratford Way YO32 . 47 A4
Stray Garth YO31 . . . . 52 B4
Straylands Gr YO31 . . 48 B1
Stray Rd YO31 . . . . . . 53 A3
STREET HOUSES . . . . 25 B1
Street La LS24 . . . . . . 32 C4
STRENSALL . . . . . . . . 11 C4
STRENSALL CAMP . . 12 A3
Strensall Comm Nature

Reserve★ YO60 . . . . 6 C1
Strensall Pk YO32 . . . 11 C2
Strensall Rd

Earswick YO32 . . . . . 42 C4
York YO32 . . . . . . . . 42 B3
Stripe La YO30 . . . . . . 39 A2
Stuart Cl 3 YO32 . . . . . 6 B1
Stuart Rd YO24 . . . . . 54 C2
Stubden Gr YO30 . . . . 45 B3
Sturdee Gr YO31 . . . . 51 C4
Summerfield Rd

YO24 . . . . . . . . . . . 59 C3
Sunningdale Cl 1

YO26 . . . . . . . . . . . 49 A2
Sunnydale 3 YO32 . . 41 C4
Sunny Way YO30 . . . . 45 B1
Surtees St YO30 . . . . . 51 A4
Sussex Cl YO10 . . . . . 58 B3
Sussex Rd YO10 . . . . . 58 B3
Sussex Way 14 YO32 11 C4
Sutherland St YO23 . . 56 A2
Sutor Ct 17 YO23 . . . 26 C3
Sutton Bridge★

YO1 . . . . . . . . . . . . 31 B1
SUTTON-ON-THE-

FOREST . . . . . . . . . . 4 B4
Sutton-on-the-Forest

CE VC Prim Sch YO61 . .4 B4
SUTTON UPON

DERWENT . . . . . . . . 31 B2
Sutton Upon Derwent

CE VC Prim Sch

YO41 . . . . . . . . . . . 31 B3
Sutton Way YO30 . . . 46 A1
Swale Ave YO30 . . . . . 45 C1
Swallows The 3 YO32 6 A1
Swan Cl YO19 . . . . . . . 35 C4
Swan Farm Ct YO19 . 35 C4
Swann St YO23 . . . . . 65 A1
Swinegate YO1 . . . . . . 65 B2
Swinegate Ct E YO1 . 65 B2
Swinsty Ct YO30 . . . . 45 B2
Sycamore Ave YO32 . 41 C1
Sycamore Cl

1 Haxby YO32 . . . . 41 C4
Skelton YO30 . . . . . . 39 B2
Sycamore Pl YO1 . . . . 41 C1
Sycamore Terr YO30 . 64 A3
Sycamore View 17

YO26 . . . . . . . . . . . 16 B2
Sykes Cl YO61 . . . . . . . .2 A4

**T**

Tadcaster Rd YO24 . . 55 B2
Tadcaster Rd

Dringhouses YO23 . . 60 A2
Tamworth Rd 3

YO30 . . . . . . . . . . . 45 C2
TANG HALL . . . . . . . . 52 B2
Tang Hall La YO31 . . . 52 C2
Tang Hall Prim Sch

YO31 . . . . . . . . . . . 52 B2
Tanner Row YO1 . . . . 65 A2
Tanner's Moat YO1 . . 65 A2

Tarbert Cres **2** YO24 59 A4
Tatton Cl YO30 ..... 45 C2
Taurus Ct YO23....... 65 A1
Teal Dr YO24 ....... 54 B1
Tedder Rd YO24 ..... 54 A2
Telford Terr **1** YO24 . 56 A3
Temple Ave YO10.... 53 A1
Temple Garth YO23.. 27 A2
Temple La YO23 ..... 27 A2
Templemead YO31 ... 47 A1
Temple Rd YO23 ..... 60 B1
Tennent Rd YO24 .... 54 A3
Tennyson Ave YO30.. 51 B4
Ten Thorn La YO26 .. 21 C3
Terrington Cl YO32 ... 6 A1
Terry Ave YO1 ....... 65 B1
Terry St YO23 ....... 56 B2
Thanet Rd YO24 ..... 54 C1
Thatchers Croft **31**
  YO23................ 26 C3
The Avenue **37** YO32 11 A1
Theresa Cl **3** YO31.. 47 B2
Thief La YO10 ....... 57 B1
Third Ave YO31 ...... 52 B2
Thirkleby Way YO10 . 53 A1
Thirlmere Dr YO31 ... 52 C3
Thomas St **2** YO10.. 54 A1
Thompson Dr **2** YO32 6 A1
Thompson Pl **6**
  YO26................ 50 A2
Thoresby Rd YO24 ... 54 A2
THORGANBY ....... 38 A1
Thorncroft **3** YO19.. 23 B4
Thornfield Ave **5**
  YO31................ 47 B1
Thornfield Dr **7**
  YO31................ 47 B1
Thornhills **10** YO32 .. 11 B2
Thorn Nook YO31 .... 47 B1
Thornton Moor Cl
  YO30................ 45 A3
Thorntree Gr YO30 .. 46 A3
Thornwood Covert **1**
  YO24................ 54 B2
Thorpe St YO23 ..... 56 A3
Tilmire Cl **2** YO10... 57 B1
Tinker La YO23 ...... 20 C3
Tithe Cl YO24 ....... 54 A2
Toby Ct YO32........ 11 C4
Toft Gn YO1 ........ 65 A2
Tollerton Rd YO30.... 8 A4
Top La YO23......... 26 C3
Toremill Cl YO32 .... 41 C1
Torridon Pl YO24 .... 59 A4
Tostig Ave YO10 ..... 49 B2
Tostig Cl **14** YO41.... 19 C3
Tower Pl YO1 ....... 65 B1
Tower St YO1 ....... 65 B1
Town End Gdns **3**
  YO32................ 10 C2
Townend St YO31.... 64 B4
TOWTHORPE ...... 12 A2
Towthorpe Moor La
  YO32................. 12 B2
Towthorpe Rd YO32 . 11 B2
Towton Ave **9** YO24. 55 B3
Trafalgar St YO23.... 56 A2
Tranby Ave YO10.... 53 C1
Treasurer's House ★
  YO31................ 64 B3
Trenchard Rd YO24 . 49 A3
Trenfield Ct YO24.... 55 B4
Trent Ave **2** YO32 .. 42 B3
Trentholme Dr **2**
  YO24................ 55 C3
Trent Way YO24 ..... 59 C4
Trevor Gr **8** YO24... 55 B3
Tribune Way YO30... 46 A3
Trinity La YO1....... 65 A2

Troon Cl **2** YO26 .... 49 A2
Troutbeck **7** YO24.. 59 B4
Troutsdale Ave YO30. 45 A3
Tudor Rd YO24 ...... 54 B3
Tudor Way YO32...... 6 B1
Tuke Ave YO10 ...... 53 A1
Turbary La YO32 .... 17 B4
Turks Head Ct YO1.. 64 C3
Turnberry Dr YO26 .. 49 A1
Turner's Croft YO10 . 57 C2
Turnmire Rd **1** YO24 55 A1
Turpin Ct YO11 ..... 65 C1
Twin Pike Way **14**
  YO32................ 10 C2
Tyn Garth YO19...... 27 C1

**U**

Ullswater YO24....... 59 C4
Undercroft **7** YO19.. 23 B4
Union Terr YO31...... 64 B4
University of York
  Heslington YO10..... 57 B2
  YO10................ 64 A3
University Rd YO10... 57 B3
Uppercroft **4** YO32.. 11 A1
Upper Hanover St **6**
  YO26................ 50 B2
UPPER HELMSLEY . 19 A4
Upper Newborough St
  **1** YO30.......... 51 B4
UPPER POPPLETON
  ..................... 16 B2
Upper Poppleton Jun
  Sch YO26 .......... 16 B2
Upper Price St YO23. 65 A1
Upper St Paul's Terr
  YO24................ 50 C1
Usher La YO32 ...... 11 B3

**V**

Vale The YO30 ....... 39 A2
Valley View YO19 .... 37 B4
Vanbrugh Dr YO10... 58 A3
Vanbrugh Way YO10. 57 C3
Vavasour Ct **10** YO23 26 C2
Vernon Ct **5** YO23.. 27 C3
Vernon Rd YO30..... 45 A3
Vesper Dr YO24 ..... 54 A4
Vesper Wlk YO32.... 42 B3
Vicarage Gdns **1**
  YO10................ 53 B1
Vicarage La YO19.... 28 A1
Vicars Cl **5** YO23... 26 C2
Victoria Ct **15** YO26. 50 B2
Victoria Farm Cl
  YO23................ 20 B3
Victoria St **1** YO23.. 65 B1
Victoria Way **2** YO32 47 B1
Victor St YO1........ 65 B1
Viking Cl **20** YO41 ... 19 C3
Viking Rd
  Stamford Bridge
    YO41.............. 19 C3
  YO26................ 49 B2
Villa Ct YO26 ....... 49 A4
Village Garth **1**
  YO32................ 11 A2
Village St YO30...... 45 A4
Village The
  Haxby YO32 ....... 11 A2
  Skelton YO30 ...... 13 B4
  Stockton on the Forest
    YO32.............. 17 C4
  Strensall YO32 .... 12 A4
Village The YO10 .... 53 B1
Villa Gr **2** YO31 .... 52 A3
Vincent Way YO24 ... 54 B1
Vine St YO23 ....... 56 B3

Vyner St YO31....... 51 B4

**W**

Waggoners Dr **20**
  YO23................ 26 C3
Waincroft **8** YO32... 11 C3
Wainers Cl YO23 .... 26 C3
Wain's Gr YO24 ..... 59 C4
Wain's Rd YO24 ..... 54 C1
Walker La YO19 ..... 54 B1
Walker La YO19 ..... 37 B4
Walkington La YO41 . 19 A1
Walmer Carr YO32... 10 C2
Walmgate YO1 ...... 65 C2
WALMGATE STRAY . 57 B2
Walney Rd YO31 .... 52 B2
Walnut Cl
  **50** Haxby YO32... 11 A2
  YO31................ 57 C2
Walpole St YO31 .... 51 C4
Walton Pl YO10...... 56 C1
Walworth St N **4**
  YO26................ 50 B2
Walworth St S **8**
  YO26................ 50 B2
Wandhill **31** YO32 ... 11 A2
Wandle The YO26.... 21 C2
Wansbeck **3** YO24 .. 59 A4
Ward Ct YO23 ....... 65 B1
Warehill La YO61..... 2 B3
WARTHILL ......... 18 B3
Warthill CK VC Prim
  Sch YO19 .......... 18 B3
Warwick St YO31..... 51 C4
Wasdale Cl YO32 .... 11 B3
Waterdale Pk YO31 .. 47 A2
Water End YO26 ..... 50 A2
Waterings **19** YO32 .. 10 C2
Water La
  **8** Clifton YO30 ... 45 C2
  Dunnington YO19 .. 23 B4
  YO30................ 50 C4
Waterman Ct **3**
  YO24................ 54 A2
Wath La YO41........ 19 B1
Watson St YO24 ..... 55 C4
Watson Terr **2** YO24 55 C4
Wattlers Cl **3** YO23 . 27 A3
Waveney Gr YO30 ... 46 A1
Waverley St YO31.... 64 C3
Waynefleet Gr **3**
  YO10................ 57 C4
Weavers Cl **1** YO26 . 26 C3
Weavers Pk **8** YO23. 26 C3
Weddall Cl YO24 .... 55 B2
Welborn Cl YO10 .... 52 C1
Welland Rise YO30 .. 49 C2
Wellesley Cl YO10 ... 45 C3
Wellington Row YO1. 65 A2
Wellington St YO10 .. 57 A4
Welton Ave YO26.... 49 C2
Welwyn Dr YO10 .... 57 A1
Wenham Rd YO24 ... 54 B1
Wenlock Dr YO19 .... 36 C3
Wenlock Terr YO10 .. 56 C2
Wensleydale Dr
  YO31................ 53 C1
Wentworth Rd YO24 . 56 A3
Wentworth Way
  YO10................ 57 B3
Werkdyke The YO1 .. 64 C3
Wesley Pl YO1....... 65 C2
West Bank YO23 .... 55 A4
West End YO19 ..... 28 A1
West End Ave YO23 . 33 B2
West End Cl **12** YO24 12 A4
Westerdale Ct **2**
  YO30................ 50 C3
Western Terr YO31 .. 46 C4
WEST FIELD ...... 21 C2

Westfield Cl **21** YO32 11 A2
Westfield Ct **19** YO23 26 C2
Westfield Dr YO10 ... 56 C1
Westfield Gr **12** YO32 10 C2
Westfield La
  Thorganby YO19..... 37 C2
  Wigginton YO32 .... 10 C2
West Field La YO26 . 16 A2
Westfield Pl
  **19** Haxby YO32..... 11 A2
  YO24................ 54 A2
Westfield Prim Com
  Sch YO24 .......... 54 A3
Westfield Rd **20**
  YO32................ 10 C2
Westholme Dr YO30 . 45 A2
Westlands Gr YO31 .. 52 B4
Westminster Bsns Ctr
  YO26................ 49 C4
Westminster Pl YO26 44 C2
Westminster Rd
  YO30................ 50 C3
West Moor La YO10 . 58 A1
West Nooks **8** YO32 11 A2
Westpit La YO32 .... 11 C4
West Thorpe YO24 .. 54 A3
Westview Cl YO26 ... 49 A4
West Wood La YO23 . 21 A1
Westwood Mews **12**
  YO19................ 23 B4
Westwood Terr YO23. 56 A2
Wetherby Rd YO26 .. 54 A4
Wharfe Dr YO24 .... 54 C1
Wharncliffe Dr
  YO30................ 45 B3
Wharton Ave YO30 .. 51 A4
Wharton Rd **8** YO31 53 C1
Wheatcroft **8** YO32 . 11 C3
Wheatfield La YO32 . 10 C2
Wheatlands Gr YO26. 49 B3
Wheatley Dr **12** YO32 11 A1
Wheelhouse The **4**
  YO30................ 39 A2
Wheelwright Cl
  **20** Copmanthorpe
  YO23................ 26 C3
  Sutton upon Derwent
    YO41.............. 31 B2
WHELDRAKE ...... 30 B1
Wheldrake CE Prim Sch
  YO19................ 30 B1
Wheldrake Ings Nature
  Reserve ★ YO19 ... 38 B4
Wheldrake La YO19.. 36 C2
Whenby Gr YO31 .... 47 B2
Whernside Ave YO31 52 C2
Whin Cl
  **3** Strensall YO32 . 12 A3
  York YO24 ......... 60 B4
Whin Garth YO24 ... 60 B4
Whinny La YO60..... 13 C4
Whin Rd YO24 ...... 60 B4
Whip-ma-whop-ma-
  gate YO1 .......... 65 C2
Whistler Cl **3** YO23 . 27 A3
Whitby Ave YO31 ... 52 C4
Whitby Dr YO31..... 52 C4
Whitecross Gdns
  YO31................ 51 C4
White Cross Rd YO31 51 C4
White Horse Cl **6**
  YO32................ 42 B2
White House Dale
  YO24................ 55 B2
White House Dr
  YO24................ 55 B2
White House Gdns **4**
  YO24................ 55 B2
White House Gr **1**
  YO41................ 31 A3
White House Rise
  YO24................ 55 B2

White Rose Ave **3**
  YO32................ 46 C4
White Rose Cl YO26 . 44 B2
Whiterose Dr YO41... 19 C3
White Rose Gr **5**
  YO32................ 46 C4
White Rose Way
  YO26................ 44 B1
Whitestone Dr YO31. 47 A3
Whitethorn Cl YO31 . 47 A3
Whitley Cl YO30 .... 45 C2
Whitley Rd YO41 .... 30 C4
Whitton Pl YO10..... 53 B1
WIGGINTON ....... 10 C2
Wigginton Prim Sch
  YO32................ 10 C2
Wigginton Rd YO31.. 64 B4
Wigginton Terr YO31 46 B1
Wilberforce Ave
  YO30................ 51 A4
Wilkinson Way **3**
  YO32................ 11 C4
Willans Gr YO26 .... 50 A1
William Plows Ave
  YO10................ 57 A3
Willis St YO10 ...... 57 A4
Willoughby Way
  YO24................ 54 A1
Willow Bank YO32... 42 A1
Willow Ct YO41...... 19 B3
Willow Glade YO32 .. 47 B4
Willow Gr
  Earswick YO32 ..... 42 C4
  York YO31.......... 52 B4
Willows The **3** YO32 12 A4
Wilstrope Gr **1**
  YO10................ 57 B2
Wilstrop Farm Rd **11**
  YO23................ 26 C2
Wilton Rise YO24.... 55 B4
Wimpole Cl **6** YO30. 47 A3
Winchester Ave **3**
  YO26................ 50 A1
Winchester Gr **1**
  YO26................ 50 A1
Windermere YO24 ... 59 C4
Windmill La YO10 ... 58 A3
Windmill Rise YO26 . 55 A4
Windmill Way **22**
  YO32................ 11 B2
Windsor Dr **2** YO32. 10 C2
Windsor Garth YO24. 54 C2
Windsor St YO23 .... 56 B2
Winscar Gr **9** YO30 . 45 A4
Winterscale Ct T01.. 56 C3
Winterscale St YO10. 56 C3
Wisker La YO32 ..... 43 B4
Witham Dr YO32 .... 42 C3
Woburn Cl YO33..... 6 A1
Woldcroft YO41 ..... 31 B3
Wolfe Ave YO31 .... 52 B2
Wolsey Dr **8** YO23 .. 27 C3
Wolsley St YO10 .... 57 A4
Wolviston Ave YO10 . 58 B4
Wood Carr YO7 ..... 11 C4
Woodcock Cl **8**
  YO32................ 11 B2
Woodford Pl **1**
  YO24................ 54 C2
Woodhouse Gr **4**
  YO31................ 52 C2
Woodland Chase
  YO30................ 46 A2
Woodland Pl YO22... 42 A1
Woodlands YO19 .... 36 A2
Woodlands Ave **11**
  YO32................ 11 A1
Woodlands Gr YO31 . 52 C2
Woodland Way YO32 42 B1
Woodlea Ave YO26 .. 49 B1
Woodlea Bank YO26. 49 C1
Woodlea Cres YO26 . 49 C1

Woodlea Gr YO26 ... 49 C1
Woodleigh Cl **2**
  YO32................ 11 C3
Woodside Ave YO31 . 52 C3
Woodsmill Quay YO1. 65 B2
Wood St YO31....... 52 A3
WOODTHORPE ..... 59 B4
Woodthorpe Prim Sch
  YO24................ 59 B4
Wood Way YO32 .... 42 C1
Woolnough Ave
  YO10................ 58 A4
Worcester Dr YO31 . 53 A2
Wordsworth Cres
  YO24................ 59 B2
Wray's Ave YO31 ... 47 A2
Wycliffe Ave YO10... 58 A3
Wydale Rd YO10 .... 53 C1
Wynam La YO41..... 31 B2

**Y**

Yarburgh Gr **2** YO26 50 A2
Yarburgh Way YO10 . 58 B4
Yearsley Cres YO31 . 51 C4
Yearsley Gr YO31 ... 47 B2
Yearsley Gr Prim Sch
  YO32................ 47 B2
Yearsley Swimming
  Pool YO31.......... 46 C1
Yew Tree Cl
  Acaster Malbis YO23 27 B1
  Rufforth YO23...... 20 B2
Yew Tree Mews
  YO19................ 53 B2
YORK ............... 64 B2
York Abbey ★ YO30 . 64 A3
York Art Gall ★ YO30. 64 B3
York Barbican Leisure
  Ctr YO10........... 65 C1
York Bridge Rd YO61 . 2 A3
York Castle Mus ★
  YO1................. 65 C1
York City Football Club
  YO30................ 64 A4
York Coll YO24 ..... 60 A3
York District Hospl
  YO31................ 46 A1
York Dungeon ★ YO1 65 B2
York La YO60........ 7 A1
York Minster ★ YO1.. 64 B3
York Model Rly ★
  YO1................. 65 A2
York Racecourse (The
  Knavesmire) ★
  YO24................ 55 C2
York Rd
  Bilbrough YO23..... 25 A3
  Dunnington YO19 .. 22 C3
  Haxby YO32 ....... 41 C4
  Naburn YO19 ...... 27 C1
  Stillingfleet YO19 .. 34 C1
  Strensall YO32 .... 11 B3
  Sutton-on-the-Forest
    YO61.............. 4 B3
York St John Coll of the
  Univ of Leeds YO10. 58 A4
Yorkshire Air Mus ★
  YO41................ 30 B4
Yorkshire Mus ★
  YO30................ 64 A3
Yorkshire Mus of
  Farming ★ YO19 ... 22 C4
York St **5** YO10 .... 23 A4
York Sta YO24....... 65 A2
York Steiner Sch
  YO10................ 56 C2

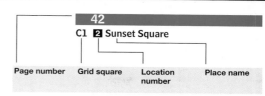

## List of numbered locations

In some busy areas of the maps it is not always possible to show the name of every place.

Where not all names will fit, some smaller places are shown by a number. If you wish to find out the name associated with a number, use this listing.

*The places in this list are also listed normally in the Index.*

| 42 |
| --- |
| C1 **2** Sunset Square |

Page number — Grid square — Location number — Place name

**2**
A4 **1** Moorlands La
**2** Green The
**3** Kyle Cl
**4** Hambleton View
**5** Church Cl
**6** Jubilee Court

**6**
A1 **1** Lakeside Gr
**2** Thompson Dr
**3** Swallows The
**4** Blacklee Cl
**5** Northfields
**6** Netherwoods
**7** Littlethorpe Cl
B1 **1** Chapman Cl
**2** Brunswick Cl
**3** Pulleyn Cl
**4** Stuart Cl
**5** Coulson Cl
**6** Cundall Cl

**10**
C2 **1** Castle Cl
**2** Windsor Dr
**3** Town End Gdns
**4** Steeple Cl
**5** Harewood Cl
**6** Delamere Cl
**7** Eton Dr
**8** Saxford Way
**9** Canterbury Cl
**10** Hambleton View
**11** Back La
**12** Westfield Gr
**13** Burrill Dr
**14** Twin Pike Way
**15** Stabler Cl
**16** Helmsley Gr
**17** Corner Cl
**18** Lancar Cl
**19** Waterings
**20** Butters Cl
**21** Corban Way
**22** Butt Hill

**11**
A1 **1** Lockey Croft
**2** Minster View
**3** Minster Cl
**4** Uppercroft
**5** Parkland Way
**6** Orchard Paddock
**7** Cherry Orch
**8** Dealtry Ave
**9** Kirkcroft
**10** Arenhall Cl
**11** Rye Cl
**12** Heslin Cl
**13** Ruddings Cl
**14** Bell Cl
**15** Chestnuts The
**16** Barley View
**17** Wheatley Dr
**18** Becks Cl
**19** Woodlands Ave
**20** Copwood Gr
**21** Meadow La
**22** Cherry Paddock
**23** Green Dike
**24** Lund Cl

**25** Stoop Cl
**26** Mancroft
**27** Hunters Cl
**28** Long Furrow
**29** Ryemoor Rd
**30** Cornwood Way
**31** Little Meadows
**32** The Avenue
**33** Holly Tree La
**34** Old Dike Lands
**35** Jubilee Ct
**36** Park Est
A2 **1** Village Garth
**2** Longcroft
**3** Ripley Gr
**4** Southlands
**5** Avenue The
**6** Redwood Dr
**7** Mulberry Dr
**8** Ash La
**9** Elm End
**10** Coppice Cl
**11** Little La
**12** Hawthorne Ave
**13** Birch La
**14** Fletcher Ct
**15** St Mary's Cl
**16** Sandy La
**17** Church La
**18** Broad Oak La
**19** Westfield Pl
**20** Westfield Rd
**21** Westfield Cl
**22** St Nicholas Way
**23** Plantation Way
**24** Middle Banks
**25** Hornsey Garth
**26** Glebe Way
**27** Forest Cl
**28** Churchfield Dr
**29** Sandyland
**30** Headland Cl
**31** Wandhill
**32** Kennedy Dr
**33** Abelton Gr
**34** Orchard Paddock
**35** Larch Way
**36** Acacia Gr
**37** Cyprus Gr
**38** Elder Cl
**39** Walnut Cl
B2 **1** Farndale Cl
**2** Sandholme
**3** Newdale
**4** Keldale
**5** Northcroft
**6** Rushwood Cl
**7** Lansdown Way
**8** Scriven Gr
**9** Woodcock Cl
**10** Falcon Cl
**11** Mallard Way
**12** Hall Rise
**13** Folks Cl
**14** Old Coppice
**15** New Forge Ct
**16** Chatsworth Dr
**17** Riversdale
**18** Netherwindings
**19** Thornhills
**20** Garths End
**21** Landings The

**22** Landing La
**23** Windmill Way
**24** Linley Ave
**25** West Nooks
C3 **1** Langton Ct
**2** Woodleigh Cl
**3** Oakhill Cres
**4** Chaldon Cl
**5** Beech Pl
**6** Wheatcroft
**7** Ryecroft
**8** Waincroft
C4 **1** Leyfield Cl
**2** Moorland Garth
**3** Wilkinson Way
**4** Fossland View
**5** Riverside Wlk
**6** Low Croft
**7** Wood Cl
**8** Adlington Cl
**9** Firbank Cl
**10** Osmington Gdns
**11** Melcombe Ave
**12** Portisham Pl
**13** Ladysmith Mews
**14** Sussex Way
**15** Pelham Pl

**12**
A3 **1** Knapton Cl
**2** Pasture Cl
**3** Whin Cl
**4** Cumbrian Ave
**5** Humber Dr
**6** Cumberland Cl
**7** St Wilfrid's Cl
**8** St Wilfrid's Rd
A4 **1** Orchard Way
**2** Middlecroft Gr
**3** Glebe Cl
**4** Station Sq
**5** Highlands Ave
**6** Oaklands
**7** Hallard Way
**8** Willows The
**9** West End Cl
**10** Oak Tree Way

**16**
B2 **1** Riverside Wlk
**2** Riverside Gdns
**3** Bankside Cl
**4** Springfield Rd
**5** Littlefield Cl
**6** Montague Wlk
**7** Pear Tree Ave
**8** Elm Tree Ave
**9** Limegarth
**10** Chantry Gap
**11** Grove Gdns
**12** Chantry Gr
**13** Chantry Ave
**14** Apple Garth
**15** Cherry Gr
**16** Sycamore View
**17** Fairway Dr
**18** Dikelands Cl
**19** Nether Way
**20** Riversvale Dr
**21** Allerton Dr
**22** School La
**23** Station Rd

**25** Beech Way
C2 **2** Little Garth
**3** Hutton Cl
**4** Nursery Rd
**5** Midway Ave
**6** Easthorpe Dr
**7** Orchard Rd
**8** Linton Rd
**9** Sandyridge
**10** Long Ridge Dr

**17**
C3 **1** Chaumont Way
**2** Marmiam Dr

**19**
C2 **1** Harolds Way
**2** Norseway
**3** Hardrada Way
C3 **1** Bridlington Rd
**2** Derwent Cl
**3** Daneswell Cl
**4** Burton Fields Rd
**5** Garrowby View
**6** Kingsway
**7** Darley Cl
**8** Wharton Rd
**9** St John's Rd
**10** Church La
**11** Egremont Cl
**12** Burton Fields Cl
**13** Heather Bank
**14** Tostig Cl
**15** Fairfax
**16** School Cl
**17** Roman Ave N
**18** Godwinsway
**19** Butts Cl
**20** Viking Cl
**21** Midgley Cl
**22** Brown Moor
**23** Furlong Rd
**24** Etty Cl

**21**
C3 **1** Bridle Way
**2** Hessay Pl
**3** Barkston Cl
**4** Bramham Gr
**5** Branton Pl
**6** Barkston Gr
**7** Barkston Ave

**23**
A4 **1** Stockhill Cl
**2** Copper Beeches The
**3** Manor Beeches The
**4** Manor Dr
**5** York St
**6** Owlwood La
**7** Owlwood Cl
**8** Curlew Glebe
B4 **1** Goose Mill
**2** Holly Tree Croft
**3** Aspen Cl
**4** Orchard Cotts
**5** Petercroft Cl
**6** Kendal Cl
**7** Undercroft
**8** Thorncroft
**9** Sawyers Wlk

**10** Coneycroft
**11** Keepers Way
**12** Westwood Mews
**13** Scaudercroft
**14** Greencroft Ct
**15** Lime Tree Mews
**16** Ox Calder Cl
**17** Greencroft La
**18** Greenside
**19** Ashdale Rd
**20** Green The
**21** Hunters Wood Way
**22** Deerstone Way
**23** Greenside Wlk
**24** Greenside Cl

**26**
C2 **1** Manor Farm Cl
**2** Church St
**3** Reygate Gr
**4** Malbys Gr
**5** Vicars Cl
**6** Deacons Ct
**7** Bellmans Croft
**8** Fairfax Croft
**9** Beadle Garth
**10** Vavasour Ct
**11** Wilstrop Farm Rd
**12** Homefield Cl
**13** Paddock Cl
**14** Barnfield Way
**15** Hobson Cl
**16** Nalton Cl
**17** Leadley Croft
**18** School La
**19** Westfield Cl
C3 **1** Link The
**2** St Nicholas Cres
**3** St Nicholas Rd
**4** St Nicholas Cl
**5** Larkfield Cl
**6** Lynwood View
**7** Rutland Cl
**8** Horseman Dr
**9** Lynwood Ave
**10** Horseman Cl
**11** Horseman Ave
**12** Millers Croft
**13** Weavers Cl
**14** Coopers Dr
**15** Drapers Croft
**16** Barbers Dr
**17** Sutor Cl
**18** Saddlers Cl
**19** Farriers Croft
**20** Waggoners Dr
**21** Hatters Cl
**22** Potters Dr
**23** Wainers Cl
**24** Faber Cl
**25** Croft Farm Cl
**26** Gardeners Cl
**27** Loriners Dr
**28** Farmers Way
**29** Wheelwright Cl
**30** Sawyer's Cres
**31** Thatchers Croft
**32** Hallcroft La
**33** Weavers Pk

**27**
A3 **1** Bowyers Cl

**2** Ropers Ct
**3** Wattlers Cl
**4** Ploughman's Cl
**5** Herdsman Dr
**6** Fletcher's Croft
**7** Ostler's Cl
**8** Whistler Cl
**9** Learmans Way
C1 **1** Main St
**2** Ferry Farm Cl
**3** Maypole Gr
**4** St Matthew's Cl
C3 **1** Harcourt Cl
**2** De Grey Pl
**3** Beech Ct
**4** Vernon Cl
**5** Wolsey Dr
**6** Melton Dr
**7** Neville Dr
**8** Lamplugh Cr
**9** Garbett Way
**10** Keble Dr
**11** Keble Pk Cres
**12** Montague Rd
**13** Orchard The

**31**
A3 **1** White House Gr
**2** Beech Cl
**3** Lorraine Ave
**4** Hillgarth Ct
**5** Dovecote Garth
**6** Beck Cl
**7** Beckside
**8** Belvoir Ave
**9** Alvin Wlk
B3 **1** Riverside Cl
**2** Riverside Gdns
**3** Church Gn
**4** Church La

**33**
B2 **1** Appleton Roebuck Prim Sch

**39**
A2 **1** Green The
**2** Meadows The
**3** Orchard View
**4** Wheelhouse The
**5** Dell The
**6** Arthur Pl

**41**
B4 **1** Ploughlands
**2** Greenway The
**3** Foxcroft
**4** Oak Tree Ct
C4 **1** Sycamore Cl
**2** Furnwood
**3** Sunnydale
**4** Pinelands
**5** Melander Gdns
**6** Rosecomb Way
**7** Milford Mews
**8** Milford Way

**42**
B2 **1** Beaulieu Cl
**2** Mendip Cl
**3** South Down Rd
**4** Grampian Cl